Buddhism in South India

Bibliotheca Indo-Buddhica Series No. 112

Buddhism in South India

D.C. AHIR

SRI SATGURU PUBLICATIONS
A DIVISION OF:
INDIAN BOOKS CENTRE
DELHI—INDIA

Published by:
SRI SATGURU PUBLICATIONS
Indological & Oriental Publishers,
A Division of
INDIAN BOOKS CENTRE
40/5, Shakti Nagar, Delhi-110007
INDIA

First Edition: Delhi-1992-
ISBN–81–7030–332-X

Typeset by:
ABC *for* DTP
6, Rajdhani Enclave, Delhi-34

Printed at:
D.K. Fine Art Press, Delhi.

PRINTED IN INDIA

Contents

Introduction

In the distant past, South India primarily meant the three kingdoms of the Chera, Chola and Pandya or the region known as the Tamil land proper, which broadly comprised the present day Tamil Nadu and Kerala. In modern usage, however, South India covers the States of Andhra Pradesh, Karnataka, Kerala, Pondicherry and Tamil Nadu - the States where the Dravidian group of languages are spoken.

Unlike other studies on the subject which primarily cover only a part of South India, this study presents a comprehensive survey of Buddhism in the whole of South India. Beginning with a brief account of the life and teachings of the Buddha, the discussion moves on to the question whether the Blessed One had sanctified the soil of South India. This is followed by the role played by Asoka in making Buddhism a living religion in South India. The subsequent five chapters trace the march of Buddhism in individual States. For better appreciation of the events, each chapter has been divided into five parts : Royal Patronage, Saints and Scholars, Sites and Shrines, the Buddhist Legacy, and the Revival Movement.

The glorious epoch of Buddhism in South India marked the efflorescence of culture in every aspect of life. The self-sacrificing Bhikkhus not only worked for their own spiritual elevation, attainment of Nirvana, but also helped and guided the vast multitude to understand and practise the sublime Dhamma based on love, compassion and equality. As a result, education became widespread, social barriers were loosened, and the Buddha Viharas became the temples of learning as well as resorts of spiritual solace for the people from all walks of life. And Buddhist art became the vehicle of cultured light dispelling the surrounding gloom.

The most important Buddhist shrines in ancient South India were : Amaravati, Nagarjunakonda, Bhattiprolu, Ghantasala and Jaggyyapetta in Andhra; Vanavasi in Karnataka; Vanji or Vanchi in Kerala; and Kanchi and Nagapattinam in Tamil Nadu. The immortal forms of art and sculpture created by the southern artists can be seen and admired in the Government Museum, Madras, and at Amaravati and Nagarjunakonda in Andhra Pradesh. The royal and public support offered to the Buddha's religion is self-evident from the large number of inscriptions left behind by the pious Buddhists at Amaravati, Nagarjunakonda and other places. It is significant that all the Brahmi epigraphs in South India are associated with the Buddhists.

The eminent Buddhist saints and scholars produced by South India include such grand personalities as Nagarajuna, the founder of the Madhyamika philosophy; Dinnaga, the great logician; Dharmakirti, the great philosopher; **Bodhidharma**, the founder of the Dhyana school of Buddhism, which became Ch'an in China and Zen in Japan; and the great Pali scholars, namely, Buddhaghosha, Buddhadatta and Dhammapala, who produced remarkable commentaries on the Tipitaka.

At one time, Buddhism became so popular and exerted so potent an influence on the minds of the people that the Brahmins felt alarmed, and in order to stem its tide, they were forced to re-adjust their religion, manners and observances so as to bring them into conformity with popular sentiments, and requirements. Their organised attempts to oust Buddhism became successful owing to the patronage of the kings, and in due course Buddhism yielded ground to the Brahmanical religion. When that happened, most of the Buddhist shrines were appropriated and re-adopted by the Hindus. Whether it is the abode of Lord Venkatesvara (Balaji) at Tirupati in Andhra Pradesh or the famous Sabarimala temple in Kerala or the holy Kamakshi Amman temple at Kanchipuram in Tamil Nadu - the story is the same every where. They were once Buddhist shrines, and even today certain Buddhist practices and traditions survive at these places. At many places in Andhra, Buddhist pillars, Ayakka Stambhas, were adopted by the Hindus to serve the purpose of the Linga. In some cases, the Hindu temples were constructed with the material taken from the Buddhist monuments by dismantling the same; the notable example in this context being the Amareshvara temple at Amaravati. Besides the shrines, much of the Buddhist culture, customs and manners were also absorbed by Hinduism. Thus, Buddhism has left a deep mark on the life and culture of South India, and this is distinctly discernible

As in North India, so also in South India, the Buddhist revival movement began at the beginning of the 20th century but its progress has been rather slow. However, Buddhism is now showing signs of vigour and vitality particularly in Andhra Pradesh and Karnataka where Buddhist population has significantly increased in the wake of the mass movement launched by Dr. B.R. Ambedkar in 1956.

D.C. AHIR

PRESENT POLITICAL MAP OF INDIA

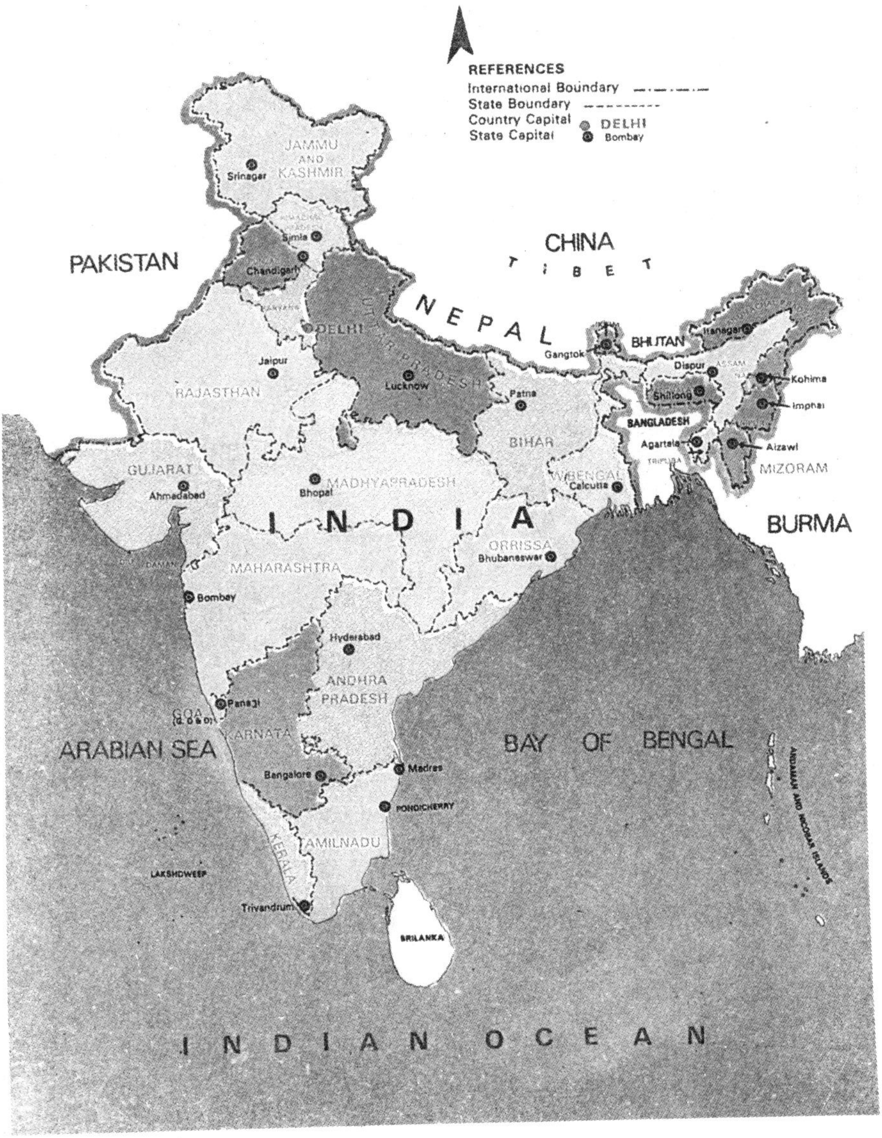

O LORD

O Lord ! You are the Wise, the Pure, the Pious and the Ancient, above all others in austerity.

O Lord ! You destroyed the evils and discarded anger; you are the Omniscient.

O Lord ! You conquered Mara; you are the Blissful; and you condemned the unholy and false ways.

O Lord ! Your feet are marked with thousand-spoked wheels I do not have thousand tongues!

How shall I praise thee?

Poet Sittalai Sattanar (2nd century A.D.)

in Manimekalai Katai V, lines, 98-105.

1

Life and Teachings of the Buddha

The Buddha was born in the sixth century BC[1] at Lumbini[2], near Kapilavastu[3], the capital city of the Sakyas, where his father was ruling. As a prince, He grew up in the midst of luxury, beauty and plenty. But slowly and slowly He was getting weary of His surroundings and was becoming more and more contemplative. Since He was not satisfied with the things around Him and wanted to discover a way out for the weal and welfare of the suffering humanity, He left his palace-home, his wife and child, and put on the garb of a mendicant at the age of twenty-nine. For six years, the *Bodhisatta* searched, scrutinized and examined in depth all the prevalent schools of thought besides practising rigid austerities and self-mortification. Ultimately, on the Full Moon day of *Vaisakha,* while meditating under the Bo-tree He attained omniscience, supreme enlightenment, at Bodh Gaya in Bihar. Thus, at the age of thirty-five, He became the Buddha, the Englightened One, the Awakened One.

The Buddha delivered His First Sermon at Sarnath[4], near, Varanasi, before the five *Parivrajakas* who had been earlier His colleagues in the forest of Uruvela. Unfolding the new path discovered by Him, the Buddha said, "Two extremes there are, O monks, which he who strives after enlightenment must avoid, which two? A life addicted to pleasure which is vulgar and worthless, and a life given to self-mortification which is painful and equally profitless". Then the Buddha enunciated the Four Noble Truths: Suffering; its causes; its cessation; and the path leading to the cessation of suffering. And added that the way to *Nibbana*, emancipation, or the path that leads to cessation of suffering, higher wisdom and peace of mind is the Noble Eightfold Path or the Middle Path. This path consists of : Right Understanding, Right Thought, Right Speech, Right Action, Right Livelihood, Right Effort, Right Mindfulness, Right Concentration.

The First Sermon of the Buddha at Sarnath is known as the '*Dhammachakra Pravartana*', the Turning of the Wheel of Law, and constituted the beginning of the Holy Spiritual and Cultural Empire of Buddhism. Annata Kondana, Bhadiyya, Vappa, Mahanama and Assaji, popularly known as *Panchvaggiya* Bhikkhus, were the first members of the Sangha founded by the Buddha. The sixth person to join the Monastic Order was Yasa or Yasoda, the son of a rich merchant of Vararasi. The Buddha gained another fifty-four disciples within a period of two months. Encouraged by the response, the Buddha decided to launch His missionary campaign. Exhorting His first sixty disciples to go and preach the Doctrine glorious, the Buddha said: "Go ye, O Bhikkhus, and wander forth for the gain of the many, for the welfare of the many, in compassion for the world, for the good, for the gain, for the welfare of the gods and men. Proclaim O Bhikkhus, the Doctrine glorious, preach ye a life of holiness, perfect and pure."

The Buddha Himself traced His steps back to Uruvela. At that time, there lived in Uruvela a sect of fire worshippers known as *Jatilas*. Their chief, Kassapa, was famous for his magical powers. When Buddha asked for shelter in his place, He was offered the room of sacred fire wherein was the fire serpent. The serpent tried to kill the Buddha but in vain. Seeing the Buddha's power and hearing the Buddha's doctrine, Kassapa and other *Jatilas* became Buddha's disciples. The two brothers of Kassapa also joined the *Sangha*.

Accompanied by these new disciples, Buddha proceeded to Rajagriha (Rajgir), the capital of King Bimbisara of Magadha, to fulfil His promise to the king. On knowing that the Sakyan Prince whom he had met years ago and tried to dissuade him from the path of holiness has since become a Buddha, King Bimbisara hastened to visit the Blessed One. He presented the Bamboo grove (*Venuvana, Veluvana*) to the Buddha and became His lay devotee. The Buddha accepted it and stayed there for some time.

There resided at that time at Rajagriha a religious teacher, Sanjaya with about 250 disciples. Among them were two young disciples, namely, Sariputta and Moggallana. Not satisfied with the teachings of Sanjaya, they were in search of something better. One day per chance Sariputta saw Assaji, one of the *Panchvaggiya* Bhikkhus, going for alms in the city of Rajagriha. Impressed by the diginfied and pleasant deportment of Assaji, Sariputta approached him and asked "friend, who is your teacher? Whose *Dhamma* do you profess?"

On knowing about the Buddha and His teachings in brief from Assaji, Sariputta told all about them to his friend, Moggallana. Soon thereafter, both of them became Buddha's disciples. Other disciples of Sanjaya also followed their example and joined the *Sangha*.

From Rajgir, the Buddha went for a time to Sarnath where He spent the first *Vasa,* Retreat during the rainy season. He then came back to Rajgir via Uruvela. In the meanwhile, His father Suddhodana sent envoy after envoy to invite the Buddha to Kapilavastu. But all failed to convey the message. Then King Suddhodana sent Kaludayi, his chief minister, to invite the Buddha to Kapilavastu. On getting the message, the Buddha agreed to go to Kapilavastu after sometime. When the Buddha, accompanied by Sariputta, Moggallana and other monks, arrived in Kapilavastu, He stopped at Banyan (*Nyagrodha*) Grove outside the city, where He was first of all worshipped by His father and other kinsmen. Next day, the Buddha accompanied by His disciples, entered the city for alms and went from house to house. When this came to the notice of King Suddhodana, he felt ashamed, and rushed to the place where the Buddha was begging. The King remonstrated the Buddha saying that such conduct was unworthy of his race. "Your's, O King is the lineage of Kings, but mine is that of the Buddhas, who have always begged for food", replied the Buddha. Later agreeing to the request of Suddhodana, the Buddha and His disciples went to the palace where they were served the best of food. After the meal, all the ladies of the palace came to pay respect to the Buddha, excepting his wife, Yasodhara. Then, accompanied by Sariputta, Buddha Himself went to the apartment of Yasodhara. There she held the feet of the Buddha and worshipped Him.

Among the Sakya princes who joined the *Sangha* were: Nanda, the son of Suddhodana by Mahaprajapati; Devadatta, Buddha's cousin; Ananda, another cousin; Anuruddha, the philosopher. Upali, the barber also joined the *Sangha*. A touching scene at Kapilavastu was the ordination of Rahula. On the seventh day, when the Buddha was on the round, Yasodhara, his wife, pointing out from the window to Rahula that Buddha was his father, asked him to go and ask for his inheritance. Rahula then went to the Buddha, and with much affection asked for his inheritance. The Buddha blessed him and marched further. But Rahula followed Him. Then the Buddha turned to Sariputta, saying; "Give him the inheritance of a holy life, which is the only treasure that I have". So Rahula was admitted to the *Sangha* when just a child. As ordination of Rahula deprived Suddhodana of all possible male heirs to his kingdom, he complained to the Buddha saying that Rahula being a child should not have been ordained without his consent. Thereupon a rule was made that no one should be admitted to the Order without the consent of his parents.

From Kapilavastu, the Buddha returned to Rajagriha. About the same time, Sudatta, a wealthy merchant of Sravasti or Savatthi, happened to visit his sister who was married to a rich merchant of Rajagriha. At the very first meeting, he became a follower of the Buddha and requested the Lord to visit Sravasti.

On returning to Sravasti, Sudatta, who because of his exemplary charity to the poor was popularly known as

Anathapindika, meaning 'the feeder of the destitute', decided to build a suitable *Vihara* for the reception of the Buddha. The only suitable site that could be found near Sravasti was the park of Prince Jeta, son of King Prasenjit. When Sudatta asked him to sell the park, Jeta demanded an exorbitant price, viz. 'as many gold pieces as will cover it'. Sudatta at once agreed, and proceeded to cover the ground with gold coins from his treasury. When all the ground, except a small piece, was covered, the prince asked Sudatta to desist, and on the uncovered ground Jeta himself erected a temple. Anathapindika also spent a huge amount to raise the magnificent *Vihara*, other shrines and monasteries. It is said that the dedication of this monastery was ceremonially gone through in the presence of the Buddha. And the Buddha, in order to commemorate the pious gifts of both, ordered that the *Vihara* should be called *"Anathapindika arama of Jetavana-Vihara"*.

The Kosala King Prasenjit or Pasendi was hitherto a supporter of the Jainas and the Ajivakas. Inspired by his son, Jeta, the King visited Buddha at Jetavana and heard a sermon which led to his conversion. Later, the King built *'Punya sala'* a hall near his Palace for the use of the Buddha.

Another important monastery erected at Sravasti for the use of the Buddha was *'Pubbarama'*. It was erected, to the east of the city, by Visakha, daughter-in-law of a rich merchant of Sravasti, namely, Migara, a follower of Jainism. Visakha, who came from a Buddhist family, persuaded her father-in-law to take refuge in the Buddha. Migara was so much impressed by the devotion and piety of Visakha that he hailed her as his mother. Therefore, she is also known as Migaramata.

The Buddha spent the fifth Ratreat at the Kutagara hall of the Mahavana grove in Vaisali. From there, He twice visited Kapilavastu, first, to settle the dispute between the Sakyas and the Koliyas regarding the waters of the Rohini in a season of drought, and second time on learning about the passing away of His father, King Suddhodhana. From there, the Buddha again returned to Vaisali. Soon thereafter, Mahaprajapati, His foster-mother, who had been earlier refused permission at Kapilavastu by the Buddha to join the *Sangha*, came to Vaisali. Covered with dust and with swollen feet, she stood outside the Kutagara hall, sad and sorrowful. Venerable Ananda saw her in that state and asked as to why she was there. She explained that she was dejected and disappointed as the Buddha had refused to grant ordination to women. Then, Ananda went to the Buddha and pleaded for the ordination of women. Thereupon, the Buddha agreed to permit ordination of Mahaprajapati, Yasodhara and other Sakyan ladies. Thus a separate Order of Nuns (*Bhikkhuni Sangha*) came to be established. Once the Order of Nuns was established, the women were on equal footing. The Buddha declared that sex was no bar to the attainment of sainthood. This ensured an honoured place for women in the society. It is significant that at least 12 of the 80 great disciples of the Buddha were women.

Thus within five years, the Buddha had gained considerable following. For the next forty years, the Blessed One travelled constantly from town to town, village to village, preaching His message of equality; of hope and peace; of kindness and compassion. As small rivulets flow towards the ocean so rushed the recluses, scholars, philosophers and lay folk towards the Buddha. The Buddha did not show any preference for any group or class of people. Irrespective of caste, colour or status, He admitted all into the *Sangha* who were willing to lead a holy life. His disciplines, both monks and lay, therefore, came from all walks of life. They included rich and poor, high and holy, and low and lowly. Here are few episodes from the life of the Buddha to show how the Blessed One went about organising His ministry:

The Buddha did not force His views on others. He encouraged the people to think for themselves rather than blindly accepting His words or those of anybody else. On a certain occasion the Lord Buddha with a number of His disciples went to the village of the Kalamas. The Kalamas assembled, and did homage to Him and said that many saints and Brahmins have at different time visited them and explained their religious tenets, declaring them to be excellent but each abused the tenets of every one else, whereupon, they, the Kalamas, became perplexed as to whose religion was right and whose wrong; but as they had heard that the Buddha taught an excellent doctrine, they begged that they might be freed from doubt, and able to learn what the truth was.

"The Lord Buddha answered, 'You were right to doubt, for after all it was a doubtful matter. I say unto all of you'.

"Do not believe in rumour, nor in anything merely because it is accepted by many or because it is based on some seemingly brilliant authority or some ancient and venerable tradition or some grand wishful thinking or because it seems extraordinary, or because it has commendable connection: only when after proper observation, analysis and reflection, it is found in accord with reason and experience and is also conducive to general good, then accept it and live upto it".

The story of Siha, Senapati of the Licchavis of Vaisali, shows remarkable tolerance of the Buddha. While welcoming him as His disciple, the Blessed One cautioned him not o antagonise his erstwhile co-religionists. Prior to his coming under the influence of the Buddha, Senapati Siha was a lavish patron of the Jainas (Nigranthas). On being requested, the Buddha accepted him as a lay disciple but urged him not to withdraw the regular alms which he had been giving to the Jaina monks.

Once the people of Alavi, a village near Sravasti, invited the Buddha and the fraternity of monks for meals. On the appointed day, the Buddha arrived at Alavi. A poor farmer, who was keen to hear the Buddha, could not, however, reach the venue in time as he had to look for a lost bull and spent the whole morning in the search of it. Though tired and oppressed with hunger, he, without going home for food, came to the place where the Buddha was seated. After saluting the Buddha, the farmer stood aside. The Buddha asked the attendants whether any food is left. On knowing that it was there, the Buddha asked them to feed the farmer. After the farmer had finished his meal, the Buddha delivered His discourse which gladdened the audience.

While dispersing the monks began to talk about this sympathetic act of the Buddha. The Blessed One then explained that 'no preaching could be understood by a person when afflicted with hunger'.

The low born Sunita tells his story like this:

"I was born in the low caste, was poor and had very little to eat. I did the low work of a scavanger. Despised and humiliated by the people, I felt frustrated. Then one day I saw the Buddha entering the city in the company of monks. I threw away my baskets and went forth to worship the Buddha, and He stood before me out of compassion. After saluting the Buddha, I stood aside and begged for ordination. The Buddha said : `Come O monk', and that was my ordination."

Sometimes the Buddha was abused and reviled. He won His opponents by patience and showing the right way to such people. One day, while going for alms from house to house in Sravasti, the Buddha approached the house of a Brahmin by the name of Aggika Bhardwaja.

The Brahmin, seeing the Blessed One coming at a distance, became angry and said: "Stay away, O Shaven headed One! There, stay, ye wretched monk! Stay away, ye miserable outcast".

When he spoke thus, the Blessed One addressed him as follows: "Do you know, O Brahmin, who an outcast is, or the things that make a person an outcast".

"No Gotama, I do not know who an outcast is. Nor indeed do I know what things make a man an outcast."

The Brahmin having responded, the Blessed One spake as follows:

"The man who is irritable, rancorous, vicious, detractive, perverted in views, and deceitful-know ye that he is an outcast".

"Whosoever in this world harms living beings, in whom there is no compassion for living beings-know ye that he is an outcast".

"An outcast is he, who hates and looks down on others".

"No one is an outcast by birth-and no one is a Brahmin by birth".

Aggika on hearing this, felt greatly ashamed for the abuse he had hurled against the Blessed One. He sought pardon from the Buddha and took refuge in the *Triple-Gem*, and became a life long devotee of the Buddha.

It is said that Ajatasatru, after the murder of his father, Bimbisara, was unable to sleep. So to seek solace, on the advice of Jivaka, the noted physician, he decided to wait on the Buddha. The King left at night by torch-light mounted on an elephant and accompanied by Jivaka and a large number of attendants. At that time, the Buddha was sitting with a large number of monks in the mango grove of Jivaka. Having gone quite far in the grove and not hearing any sound, the king was seized with a sudden fear, and said to Jivaka, "you are playing me no tricks? You are not betraying me to my foes? How can it be that there should be no sound at all, not a sneeze, nor a cough, in so large an assembly." Jivaka assured him that there was no mischief afoot: "Go on, O king, go straight on. There in the pavilion hall the lamps are burning, and that is the Buddha sitting against the middle pillar, facing the east, with the Bhikkhus around Him." And when the king looked at the assembly seated in perfect silence, calm as a clear lake, he became at ease, and wished that `his son might have such calm'. In the dialogue that follows the Buddha discourses on the fruits of the life of a recluse. At the end of discourse Ajatasatru seeks pardon for his past sins and promises to follow the *Dhamma* in future.

By the time, Buddha was about to lay down His mortal body, He had become popular with every section of society and had thousands of devout followers around Him. In fact, the people vied with one another in inviting the Buddha for a meal. When Ambapali, the courtesan of Vaisali, invited the Lord and His Bhikkhus for a forenoon meal at her residence, the Buddha accepted her invitation. On her way back she met the Licchavi nobles who had also come to invite the Buddha but were forestalled by Ambapali. They entreated Ambapali and offered her a price for giving up the invitation but she politely declined on the plea that after waiting for a long time she had got the chance and would not like to miss this golden opportunity. After the meals, Ambapali donated her *Ambavana* (Mango-grove) for the residence of the monks.

Leaving Vaisali, the Buddha headed for Kushinara, His last resting place. Touring the countryside, and passing through the city of Pava, the Buddha, accompanied by Ananda, arrived at the *Sala* grove of the Mallas on the bank of river Hiranyavati in the vicinity of Kushinara. Then, the Blessed One asked Ananda to prepare for him a bed between the twin *sal* trees, with the head to the north, as He was weary, and wanted to rest. Ananda did the Lord's bidding, and the Buddha lay down on the bed so prepared. Then a message was sent to the Mallas of Kushinara that the Blessed One had arrived there and would pass away in the last watch of the night. So informed, the Mallas came in large numbers to the *Sal* grove to have the last darshan of the Buddha.

The last few hours were spent by the Buddha in useful instructions to the *bhikkhus*. Finding Ananda lamenting bitterly, the Blessed One consoled him gently, saying, "Do not weep. do not despair, Ananda. From all that one loves, one must part, How could it be that what is born, what is subject to decay, should not pass. It may be Ananda, that you were thinking, "Gone is the Master; we have no longer a Master". But you must not so regard it, O Ananda. The *Dhamma* taught by me, shall be your master when I am gone."

Then turning to the bhikkhus, the Buddha gave His final exhortation: "Behold, O Monks, I do remind ye, `Subject to decay are all component things; work out your deliverance with earnestness Be ye lamps unto yourself".

These were the last words of the Blessed Buddha. Thus preaching, the Great Buddha passed into *Mahaparinirvana* at the age of eighty on the Full Moon day of *Vaisakha* at Kushinara (in district Deoria, Uttar Pradesh).

TEACHINGS

The fountainhead of the Buddha's Teachings is the Noble Eighfold Path. It is the path to *Nirvana*. The first step on the royal road to *Nibbana* or *Nirvana* is the observance of the Five Precepts, *Panca Sila*, which are the core of Morality in Buddhism. The Five Precepts, viz. Not to injure or kill; Not to steal;, Not to indulge in lust; Not to speak untruth; Not to take intoxicants, are in essence the combination of Right Speech, Right Action and Right Livelihood. The diligence observance of the Five Precepts (*Panca Sila*) is the best way to avoid all sin and to purify one's mind. The second step on the road to *Nibbana* is that of concentration (*Samadhi*) which includes Right Effort, Right Mind-fulness and Right Concentration. By Right Effort is to be understood a vigorous mental application by which a person, on the one hand, avoids and overcomes all evil thoughts, and on the other hand, develops and maintains good thoughts and urges. Right Mindfulness means constant wakefulness of the mind: an alert awareness or contemplation of all bodily actions or movements. And Right Concentration is the practice of meditation or taming the mind which ultimately leads to *Nirvana*. Having attained perfection in *Samadhi*, one reaches the final stage of Wisdom (*Panna*); he has clear understanding of all the unwholesome actions, which are rooted in greed (*lobha*), hatred (*dosa*) and delusion (*moha*) as well as the wholesome actions. His mind becomes pure, is free from lust, free from ill-will; is full of kindness and compassion. He has reached his goal, and is on the threshold of *Nirvana*.

Prior to the advent of the Buddha, there were two prominent cults holding the minds of the Indian people. While the Brahmins sought salvation and deliverance by resorting to bloody sacrifices, some others substituted sacrifices by self-mortification, and gave hardships to the body in the hope of getting rewards in the future. The Buddha considered both these cults as imperfect, incomplete, and not conducive to the welfare of man. Discarding both these cults, therefore, Lord Buddha laid emphasis on ethics and morality, and impressed upon the people to live righteously. He exhorted them to cross the ocean of *samsara* by doing good to others instead of harming others or harming one's own self. He said the way to *Nirvana* is through self-control, self-restraint, and elimination of passion. Hence, unlike the other religions the content of which consists of God, soul, prayers, rituals, ceremonies, sacrifices and self-mortification, spiritual progress in Buddhism is dependent on self-purification which can be achieved by leading a moral life through self-discipline, self-control.

Anicca, Dukkha and *Anatta,* better known as the 'Three Characteristics' form the essential basis of the Buddha's Teachings. Suffering, *dukkha,* is the First Noble Truth taught by the Buddha. The *Anicca,* impermanence, transience or transitoriness doctrine implies that in this world all things are changing, are in a perpetual flux. There is nothing, either organic or inorganic, which is permanent or stable, unchanging or everlasting. In other words, all conditioned things or processes are transient or impermanent (*sabbe sankhara anicca*). Since change is inherent in everything, the Buddha denies the concept of a permanent soul. According to Him, there is nothing permanent, unchanging entity in the human body which can be called soul or self.

One of the fundamental teachings of the Buddha is that in this world 'nothing happens' 'without a cause'. This principle of 'cause' and 'effect' teaching the conditionality and dependent nature of all physical and mental phenomena, is known as 'Causation' or 'Dependent Origination' (*the Paticca Samuppada*). This doctrine shows that the whole world is subject to the law of cause and effect or action and reaction. There is nothing in the universe that is causeless and unconditioned. The formula of Dependent Origination has twelve factors, and is primarily used to explain the process of re-birth. While the Buddha denied the existence of a permanent soul or ego yet He accepted the doctrine of re-birth. But the theory of re-birth in Buddhism is fundamentally different from the theory of 'transmigration of soul' in Hinduism. According to the Buddha, a being is combination of five aggregates consisting of Mind and Matter (*Nama and Rupa*). And the living being is conditioned by *Kamma* - actions directed by the will. As long as there is this *Kamma* force, there is rebirth. "Reap as you sow", says the Buddha. In other words, Man shapes his own destiny. It all depends on him whether to create painful, pleasurable or blissful life. Good deeds will naturally result in good fortune and happiness, and the bad deeds otherwise. In brief, we ourselves are responsible for our own happiness and missery. We are architects of our fate. The Buddha did not believe that the Stars can change the course of life. His view was that 'self effort' not 'stars' can mould one's destiny.

The Vedic India was unware of the ethics of equality and universal brotherhood. According to the Purusha Sukta of the Rig Veda, the Brahmins came from the mouth, Kshatriyas from the arms, Vaishyas from the thighs, and Sudras from the feet of Brahma, the Creator. This society based on the mythical origin was known as *Chaturvarna* and was regulated by the principle of graded inequality; the Brahmins being at the top, followed by Kshatriyas, Vaishyas and Sudras in descending order. This rule of graded indequality regulated their rights and privileges as well. Even the punishments for secular offences were based on the principle of inequality, the Brahmins always getting the minimum and the Sudras the maximum punishments. Thus the entire social structure was based on the principle of inequality.

The Buddha revolted against such oppressive social laws and condemned caste-system. He challenged the divine origin of the caste, and showed the hollowness of the claim of the Brahmins of having been born from the mouth of Brahma. He also refuted the Brahmin claim that only they could attain spiritual virtues, and asserted that a man of any caste, colour or creed can develop in his heart such virtues. He further said: "Let no person, whether man or woman, whatever be his or her socio-economic background, be hindered from reaching the highest perfection, which is every-one's right and within every-one's reach and, more than that, is achievable by dint of one's own ceaseless striving, unaided by any divine or supernatural agent."

The Enlightened One further pointed out that all human beings were alike and to divide them artificially was a folly. In the Vesettha Sutta, He says that in the case of animal life there are different varieties based on different essential characteristics. So is the case with plant life. But there do not exist such differences which justify classification of human beings into water-tight compartments as all men are one and the same in their essential characteristics. Therefore, the Buddha asserted in a forceful manner that worth, based on deeds, rather than birth, an accidental thing, should be the measure of man. He also took concrete steps to eradicate the evil of caste. These steps were: exposing the myth of hereditary superiority claimed by the Brahmins; encouraging the down-trodden by dining at their houses; and accepting the low and lowly as equal members of the Sangha. Exhorting the Bhikkhus to forget their caste labels, the Buddha once said, 'Just, O brethren, as the great rivers - Ganga, Yamuna, Aciravati, Saraswati and Mahi when they have fallen into the great ocean, lose their different names and are known as the great ocean - Just so, O brethren, do these four castes - Kshatriyas, Brahmins, Vaishyas and Sudras - when they begin to follow the doctrine and discipline as propounded by the *Tathagata*, they renounce different names of castes and rank, and become members of one and the same society".

The Buddha gave courage to man to fight the dogmatism, the formalism and the rigid ritualism. By His most systematic, scientific and bold philosophy He tried to take man's mind away from the pursuit of selfish ends by emphasizing the utter unreality of this life. How bold was the Buddha can be well judged from the fact that in order or fulfil His Mission He had to deny entirely the traditional gods, conventional religious beliefs, institutions and customs. After demolishing all that was undesirable and hinderance in the pursuit of *Dhamma*, the Lord proceeded further and initiated a new cult based on morality, equality, reason and self-help. He declared that the creative urge within us needs no outside help to secure the fruition and fulfilment of life's mission on Earth. His last words very clearly testify this call for concerted effort by the mankind. He says, "Be ye lamps unto yourselves. Rely on yourselves and do not rely on external help. Hold fast to truth as a lamp. Seek salvation alone in the truth".

Gautama the Buddha was the First Teacher in this world who diverted the attention of the scholars and saints, philosophers and rulers from the sky, and compelled them to see around them and work for the welfare of the masses. Uptill now the approach to the problem of liberation was individualistic and the seeker did not at all care for his brethren but the Blessed One gave a new turn to this approach and made social service as a prerequisite to the attainment of *Nirvana*. Hitherto the eyes of the people were always looking for some god or goddess for blessings. The Buddha brought all these gods and goddesses down to the earth and made them inferior to man. He said, 'gods will have to take birth as human beings before they can attain *Nirvana*.' This approach of the Buddha was so original and novel that it revolutionised the ideas of the people. It paved the way for the new values of life and new principles of life.

Notes and References

1. According to tradition, the Buddha was born in 624-23 BC and attained Mahaparinirvana in 544 BC. But the historians generally accept 563 and 483 BC as the dates of His birth and Mahaparinivana.

2. Lumbini is in Nepal, just 10 km from the Indo-Nepalese border touching district Basti in Uttar Pradesh.

3. Kapilavastu has since been identified with Piprahwa in district Basti in Uttar Pradesh. The relics of the Buddha discovered from the Piprahwa Stupa in 1972 by K.M. Srivastava of the Archaeological Survey of India are now preserved in the National Museum, New Delhi.

4. The life of the Buddha is largely based on Pali sources.

2

Buddha's Visit to South India

The Turning of the Wheel of Law at Sarnath in Uttar Pradesh constituted the beginning of the Holy Spiritual and Cultural Empire of Buddhism. The *Panchvaggiya* Bhikkhus, Annata Kondana, Bhadiya, Vapa, Mahanama and Assaji, were the first five members of the Bhikkhu *Sangha* founded by the Buddha. The sixth person to join the Monastic Order was Yasa, the son of a rich merchant of Varanasi (Banaras). Within a couple of months, the Buddha gained another fifty-four disciples, thus making a total of sixty monks. Encouraged by the response to His doctrine, the Blessed One decided to launch His missionary compaign. Exhorting His first sixty disciples to go and preach the Doctrine glorious, the Buddha said: "Go Ye, O Bhikkhus, and wander fourth for the gain of the many, for the welfare of the many, in compassion for the world, for the good, for the gain, for the welfare of the gods and men. Proclaim O Bhikkhus the Doctrine glorious, preach ye a life of holiness, perfect and pure".

For the next 45 years, the Buddha travelled constantly from town to town, village to village preaching His message of love and piety. As small rivulets flow towards the ocean so rushed the recluses, scholars, philosophers and layfolk towards the Buddha. The Buddha did not show any preference for any group or class of people. Irrespective of caste, colour or status, He admitted all into the *Sangha* who were willing to lead a holy life. His disciples, both monks and lay, therefore, came from all walks of life. They included rich and poor, high and holy, and low and lowly. All had equal opportunity to enter and walk the path, and attain the blessed state of *Nirvana*.

After having led for 45 years a very strenuous and selfless life in teaching the beauty of charity, the joy of renunciation, the need for simplicity and equality, the Great Buddha passed into *Mahaparinirvana* at the age of 80, at Kushinara in Uttar Pradesh

The field of missionary activity of the Lord Buddha , as revealed by the canonical sources, was mainly confined to the North, and North-East India. There is no direct evidence forthcoming to show that the Blessed Buddha ever went as far as the present day Madras during His preaching tours. However, tradition associates the Buddha with atleast two places in modern Tamil Nadu. These are: Kanchipuram and Buddhavedu.

Kanchipuram, about sixty kilometers from Madras, is the most ancient and historic city in Tamil Nadu. Lord Buddha is said to have visited Kanchipuram more than once. Such a tradition was prevalent at the time of Asoka (273-232 BC), the first Buddhist Emperor, who is credited with the erection of a commemorative stupa on the spot where the Buddha had rested during His visit to Kanchi. Hiuen Tsang, the celebrated Chinese pilgrim, who visited Kanchipuram in AD 640, says[1]:

"This country (Dravida) is about 6000 li in circuit; the capital of the country is called Kanchipura (Kin-chi-pu-lo), and is about 30 li round .... Tathagata in olden days, when living in the world, frequented this country much; he preached the law here and converted men, and therefore Asoka-raja built stupas over all the sacred spots where these traces exist."

Hiuen Tsang further says:

"To the south of the city not a great way is a large *sangharama* in which men of the same sort, renowned for talent and learning, assemble and stop. There is a stupa about 100 feet high which was built by Asokaraja. Here, Tathagata, dwelling in old days, repeated the law and subdued the heretics, and converted both men and Devas in great number."

Besides Kanchipuram or Conjeevaram, another site in Tamil Nadu traditionally associated with the Buddha is Buddhavedu, a small village, just 21 kilometers from Madras city. It is said that the Buddha rested here when He went to the South. The archaeological evidence since discovered at Buddhavedu includes a Buddha image, a Bodhi tree, and the remains of a monastery. According to an inscription discovered on the site, the village had been dedicated to the Buddhist *Sangha* during the reign of the Rajaraja Chola in the tenth century AD. Evidently, the site had a hoary Buddhist past.

According to the story of Bavari and his sixteen disciples found in the introductory sutta of the *Parayanavagga*[2] of the *Sutta-Nipata,* an oldest text of the Pali Tipitaka, the Buddha's Teachings had reached Andhra during the life time of the Blessed One. It is said that Bavari, a Brahmin teacher, who had his ashram on the banks of river Godavari near Aḷaka in the Assaka country, once arranged to perform a major *yajna*. The ceremony was upset by another Brahmin who came after the gifts had been distributed and cursed Bavari for not having anything for him. On knowing that the Buddha is the only sage capable of foiling the curse, Bavari sent his sixteen disciples to question the Blessed One. The disciples of Bavari accordingly came to the north, and met the Buddha at the Stone *Chaitya* outside the city of Rajagaha, modern Rajgir in Bihar. The questions put by them and the Blessed One's answers thereto are preserved in the subsequent suttas of the *Paryanavagga,* named after the disciples[3] of Bavari.

The ancient Assaka country has been identified[4] by the scholars with the present day Aurungabad-Nanded region of Maharashtra and Nizamabad area of Andhra Pradesh. Thus, Buddhism had reached Andhra during the life time of the Buddha and from Andhra it penetrated into Tamil Nadu.

Notes and References

1. Samuel Beal, SI-YU-KI Buddhist Records of the Western World - translated from the Chinese of Hiuen Tsiang. In Two Volumes (Bound in One), Delhi Reprint, 1981, Volume II, pp. 228-230.

2. V. Fausball, The Sacred Books of the East, Part II, The Sutta Nipata - translated from Pali, Delhi Reprint, 1973, p. 184-213.

3. Ibid. The names of the 16 disciples of Bavari were : Ajita, Tissametteyya, Punnaka, Mettagu, Dhotaka, Upasiva, Nanda, Hemaka, Todeyya, Kappa, Jatukani, Bhadravuddha, Udaya, Posala, Mogharajan and Pingiya.

4. D.D. Kosambi, The Culture and Civilization of Ancient India, New Delhi, 1976 edition, pp. 111-112, says : "The Kosalan brahmin Bavari had left the capital (Savatthi) to go down the southern trade route (*dakshinapattha,* the modern Deccan). He settled with a few young disciples at the junction of the Mula and Godavari rivers, in the territory of the Assakas (the Horse People, the tribe that later developed into the Satavahanas).

3

Asoka and South India

One of the greatest events in Indian history took place in 322 BC. This was the founding of the Mauryan Empire by Chandragupta Maurya after defeating the last Nanda king of Magadha. Later, Chandragupta Maurya expanded his empire in all directions, and by the time he died in 298 BC, the Mauryan Empire included the whole of India, excluding Kalinga and the territories beyond Mysore in the south. It also included Afghanistan. Thus, for the first time in Indian history, a greater part of India was brought under the control of a single ruler. Chandragupta was succeeded by his son, Bindusara, who ruled from 298-274 BC, and maintained the vast Mauryan empire.

Asoka, son of Bindusara, ascended the Magadhan throne in 273 BC, after his father's demise. His coronation took place in 269 BC. Asoka had inherited a well-established empire, founded by his grandfather, Chandragupta. To this vast empire, he added Kalinga, modern Orissa, which he conquered after a bloody war in about BC 262. The large scale massacre in the Kalinga war deeply influenced the mind of Asoka and brought revolution in his character. With this event, his outlook, both in his personal and public life, changed. Consequently, he was drawn to the sublime Teachings of the Lord Buddha. Asoka himself says : "Directly after the conquest of the Kalingas, the beloved of the gods became keen in the pursuit of *Dhamma*, love of *Dhamma* and inculcation of *Dhamma*. This is due to the repentence of the beloved of the gods on having conquered the country of the Kalingas".

After adopting the Buddha Dhamma as his guide, Asoka declared that henceforth he would prefer *'Dhamma-Vijaya'* to *'Rajya-Vijaya'*. In other words, he took a vow to abjure violence and to win the hearts of the people, both inside and outside the borders of his empire, by persuation and love, instead of by the use of force and sword. "The chiefest conquest is not that by arms but by *Dhamma* (*Dhamma Vijaya*)", he said. Consequently, Asoka dedicated all his energies, power and pelf to the cause of *Dhamma-Vijaya*. What he desired to achieve, and what he was able to achieve is well-documented in the edicts and inscriptions of Asoka on the rocks and pillars which have since been discovered at 40 places in India (34), Nepal (2), Pakisatan (2), and Afghanistan (2).

To what extent the Mauryan Empire extended in the South has been a matter of discussion among the scholars. It is generally agreed that Andhra Pradesh and a major part of Karnataka formed part of the Mauryan Empire. However, the question whether this entire region was conquered by Chandragupta or a part of it was annexed by Asoka is a matter on which opinions differ. The latest historical evidence, which has surfaced by way of an Asokan rock edict at Sannati in Gulbraga district of Karnataka, suggests that Asoka may have annexed the northern part of Karnataka and adjoining portions of Andhra. This fragmentary Asokan rock edict was discovered in January 1989, by the staff of the Archaeological Survey of India, Hyderabad Circle on the backside of the granite stone slab which was used as a *pitha* (base) for fixing up an image of Mahakali in the ruined Kalikamba shrine in the Chandralamba temple complex built during the eighth or ninth century AD. The slab contains a major part of separate Rock Edict II, and also a very fragmentary portion of Separate Rock Edict I. The contents of Separata Rock Edict II are similar in content and style to the Kalinga Rock Edict in Orissa wherein Asoka endeavours to pacify the people of Kalinga conquered by him, and goes on to say that "All men are my children. Just as, in regard to my own children, I desire that they may be provided by me with all kinds of welfare and happiness in this world and in the next, the same I desire in respect of all men".

The text and translation of the Asokan Separate Rock Edict II discovered at Sannathi, as given by K.V. Ramesh, is as follows[1]:

TEXT

1. .... anuvig (i)......
2. .... sevu cha sukhameva cha labh (ev)u...
3. .... yena cha hevaṁ pāpunevu rājā ne kham (i)....
4. ye khamitave mamaṁ nimitaṁ v dhammaṁ clarevū hida .....
5. cha paralokaṁ cha ārādhayevu (1*) etyāya cha athaya hakaṁ tuphe....
6. anusāsāmi aṇamṇe hakaṁ tupheṇi anusāsitu chhamadam cha ditu
7. yāhi mama dhiti paṭiṁṇa cha a(cha)lā (1*) sāti hevaṁ katu kaṁme charitaviye
8. āsvāsetaviyā cha to yena cha to hevaṁ pāpunevu athā pita hevaṁ
9. (ne) rājā yathā cha atānām anukaṁpati hevaṁ apheni ya (tha) (1*)
10. chakaṁ pajā hevaṁ ma(yi) se hakaṁ tupheni anusāsitu chhamdam cha
11. ditu desāvutike etasi athasi hohāmi (1*) alaṁ hi tuphe asvasanaye
12. hita-sukhāye cha tesaṁ hidalokika pāralokikāye (1*) etaṁ cha hevaṁ
13. karaṁtaṁ svag (am cha) ārodhesātha mama cha anāniyaṁ ehatha (1*) etā-
14. .... ya iyaṁ lipi hida likhitā atha mahāmātā sāsvataṁ
15. .... yujevu āsvāsasnāya dhamma-charanāya cha aṁtā..
16. ...(1*)... cha lipi anuchātumāsi sota (vi) yā (ti) seni (1*) amtarapi

17. .... hi khanasi khanasi..... taviyā (1*) hevam
18. .... ghata saṁpati.....

TRANSLATION

1. ....
2. ...., and may obtain only happiness.....
3. .... and may learn that the king will (forgive)...
4. .... what can be forgiven; they may because of me practise morality; .... in this (world).
5. .... obtain happiness.... and in the other world. And for this purpose I am instructing you....

6-10. That I may discharge the debt by this and inform you of my will (that is) of my unshakable resolution and vow. Therefore you must thus engage in hard work and inspire them with confidence and exhort them whereby they will realize that the king is unto them like a father, that he is as considerate towards them as he is unto his own self, that they are to the king like his own children.

10-11. Having thus instructed you and informed you of my will I shall appoint officers all over the land for this purpose.

11-12. Indeed you are able to inspire them with confidence for their welfare and confidence in this world and in the other world.

12-13. By acting thus you will ascend to heaven and you will discharge what you owe me.

13-15. For the following (purpose) has this edict been written here so that the *mahamatras* may at all times strive to inspire the borders with confidence and exhort them to practise morality.

16. And this edict must be heard every four months on (the day of) Tishya.

16-17. Even in between it may be (listened to) every now and then.

18 ....

Having regard to the contents of this rock edict, the Archaeological Survey of India (ASI), says[2], "With the recent discovery of rock edict at Sannati in Gulbarga district of Karnataka, historians can with authority say that Asoka had annexed northern part of Karnataka and adjoining portions of 'Andhra Desa' during the third century B.C."

On the front portion of the slab have survived some fragments of the Major Rock Edicts XII and XIV. Apparently, the slab had originally all the Fourteen Rock Edicts as at other places. According to the Archaeological Survey of India, Hyderabad, this rock edict is identical in content and script, style and language to the major rock edict at Yerragudi (Erragudi) in district Kurnool of Andhra Pradesh. As elsewhere, here too, Rock Edict XII speaks of the virtues of religious tolerance. In Rock Edict XIV, Asoka offers apology for any inadequacies in the presentation of his edicts on morality which may be either due to local anathema or the fault of the writer.

So far as Tamil Nadu is concerned, a part of it, the area around Kanchipuram, known as Tondaimandalam in ancient days, may have formed part of the Mauryan empire. As already noticed in Chapter II, Lord Buddha is said to have visited Kanchipuram, and to commemorate this event, Asoka had erected a *Stupa* at Kanchipuram. This *stupa* was still standing when Hiuen Tsang, the Chinese pilgrim, visited Kanchi in 640 AD. He says[3], "To the south of the city not a great way is a large *sangharama* in which men of the same sort, renowned for talent and learning, assemble and stop. There is a stupa about 100 feet high which was built by Asokaraja. Here, Tathagata, dwelling in old days, repeated the law and subdued the heretics, and converted both men and devas in great number."

Since Asoka the Great erected stupas and pillars or engraved rock edicts only within his empire, and not in foreign territories, Kanchipuram must have formed part of the Mauryan empire. There is sufficient other evidence also to confirm this inference. In the Kurram Plates[4] of Paramesvaravarman I (670-691 AD), which describe the military achievements of this Pallava king, there is mention of a king named Asokavarman as one of the earliest rulers of Kanchi. Apparently, the king referred to herein is Asoka Maurya. K.A. Nilakanta Sastri opines that this reference may "well be a relic of Mauryan rule in the South[5]". At another place, he says[6], "how much further south the empire of the Mauryas extended can only be conjectured; it seems not unlikely that a part of the Tondaimandalam was included in it." According to Prof. R. Sathianatha Aiyer[7], "the Pallavas belonged to Tondaimandalam which was a province (with Kanchi as capital) of the Asokan empire. He takes the word Pallavas to be a variant of Palada referred to in the Asokan edicts. The latter were identical with the Pulindas who were included among the Southern-most subject peoples of the Mauryan emperor. The association of Pulindas with Tondaimandalam is evident from the names Pulinadu and Puliyar Kottam, two ancient divisions of this region."

In pursuance of his policy of *Dhamma-Vijaya* (Moral Conquest), Asoka launched a concerted compaign to mitigate the suffering of the people, rather all living beings, in his empire. He undertook the provision of public works of utility on such a large scale which was never witnessed before in India. With a view to making travelling comfortable and safe, he planted shady trees on highways, dug wells and constructed rest houses at appropriate places. He opened hospitals for men and animals alike. He also laid botanical gardens for the rare medicinal plants and healing shrubs (R.E. II). In order to improve the social conditions, Asoka ordered abolition of : sacrificial slaughter of animals; *samajas* (merry making of a kind, accompanied by animal fights and feasting with consumption of meat etc.); hunting and other similar amusements (R.E. I.). He devoted all his time and energy to the affairs of State, and made arrangements to receive reports on state business at all hours. Asoka thus spared no efforts for the weal and happiness of his subjects. He says, "There is no greater duty for him than doing good to all." (R.E. VI). The benevolent Asoka goes on to say: "All men are my children. I wish happiness and welfare to all men, as I would wish to my own children." (Separate Rock Edict-Dhauli Text).

Asoka was even anxious to promote the welfare and happiness of the people living beyond his domain and he organised missionary work in the foreign countries, and made arrangements for the supply of medical aid and other facilities for the people not directly under him. In the second major rock edict found at Girnar in Gujarat, Asoka tells us how he had made arrangements for the medical care and provided other amenities to the people living in the southern kingdoms not directly under his domain, in Ceylon and in the Greek kingdoms. The Edict reads as follows[8]:

"Everywhere in the empire of the Beloved of the Gods, the king Piyadassi, and even in the lands on its frontiers, those of the Cholas, Pandyas, Satyaputras, Keralputras, and as far as Ceylon, and of the Greek named Anticochus and of those kings who are neighbours of that Antichus, everywhere the two medical services of the Beloved of the Gods, the king Piyadassi, have been provided. These consist of the medical care of men and the care of animals. Medicinal herbs whether they did not grow useful to man or beast, have been brought and planted wherever they did not grow; similarly, roots and fruit have been brought and planted wherever they did not grow. Along the roads, wells have been dug and trees planted for the use of men and beasts."

The three southern kingdoms referred to above are the well-known kingdoms of Chola (the Coromandel Coast), the Pandya (the southern tip of the Peninsula), and Kerala or Chera (Malabar), which lay on the borders of the Mauryan Empire. The fourth southern kingdom, that of the Satyaputra, referred to in the Edict, had defied identification for a long time. However, recent discovery of a Tamil-Brahmi inscription[9] in district South Arcot of Tamil Nadu commemorating a gift by *"Atiyan Naduman Anji, the Satyaputra"* has thrown valuable light on this vexed problem. Beside confirming the correctness of the Asokan Edict, it also confirms beyond doubt that Asoka had friendly relations with all the southern kingdoms.

Asoka modelled his administration on the basis of the *Dhamma* tenets and emphasized the supermacy of the moral laws. To begin with, he commanded all his officers to tour the country-side atleast once in five years for missionary work among the masses (R.E. III). Later, he created a separate Department of Missionary Service under the Officers styled as *Dhamma-Mahamataras,* Ministers of Religion or Morals, for propagation of piety among his subjects

(R.E.V.). He also held regular religious conferences and discussions on the *Dhamma*; and organised religious shows and processions (R.E.V.) Further, Asoka initiated his own pious tours or 'pilgrimages of piety' (*dhamma-yatra*) to the sacred Buddhist shrines (R.E. VIII). He went on pilgrimage to Lumbini, the birth place of the Buddha, to *Sambodhi*, the seat of Buddha's enlightenment, to Sarnath, the site of His First Sermon, to Kushinara, the scene of Buddha's *Maha-parinirvana*, and other holy places sanctified by the Buddha. Asoka also opened *Dhamma* centres and endeavoured to popularise the practice of Buddhist meditation (*Vipassana*).

In order to give impetus to the propagation of *Dhamma*, Asoka is said to have built 84,000 stupas throughout his empire. In Kashmir alone, he is said to have built 500 monasteries. He is also said to have given the whole of Kashmir for the benefit of the Buddhist *Sangha*. Asoka is also credited with the founding of Srinagar, the capital of Kashmir. Another city founded by him was Deo-Patan (Deva-patana) in Nepal. As a result of all this, the sound of '*Dhammaghosha*' or '*dhamma-drum*' reverberated throughout his empire (R.E. IV.), and the *Dhamma* spread far and wide.

With his systematic and energetic efforts, Asoka took out the gospel of the Buddha from the caves and monasteries and made it a world religion. But for Asoka, Buddhism would not have perhaps witnessed the missionary work which he inspired and initiated. Asoka's missionary spirit was, therefore, responsible for the spread of Buddhism in Sir Lanka, Burma and other countries around.

Asoka speaks of his missionary work in two edicts. In Rock Edict V, he says[10], "These officers (*Dhamma-Mahamatras*) are occupied with all the religious sects for the establishment of *Dhamma* and for the promotion of *Dhamma* as well as for the welfare and happiness of those who are devoted to *Dhamma* even among the Yavanas, Kambojas and Gandharas, the Rashtrikas and Paitryantikas and the other people dwelling about the western borders of my dominions". Again in Rock Edict XIII, he says[11], "So, what is conquest through *Dhamma* is now considered to be the best conquest has been achieved by the Beloved of the Gods not only here in his own dominions but also in the territories bordering on his dominions as far away as at the distance of six hundred Yojanas (about 1500 mile), where the Yavana king named Antiyoka is ruling and where, beyond the kingdom of the said Antiyoka, four other kings named Turamaya, Antikini, Maka and Alikaundra are also ruling, and towards the south, where the Cholas and Pandya are living as far as Tamraparni (Sri Lanka)".

In the same edict, Asoka goes on to say[12], "Likewise here in the imperial territories among the Greeks, Kambojas, Nabhakas and Nabhapanktis, Bhojas and Pitinikas, Andhras and Parindas (Pulindas), everywhere the people follow the Beloved of the Gods' instructions in *Dhamma*. Even where the envoys of the beloved of the Gods have not gone, people hear of his conduct according to *Dhamma*, his precepts and his instructions in *Dhamma*, and they follow *Dhamma* and will continue to follow it".

Asoka sent missionaries to spread the *Dhamma* in the five foreign kingdoms of Syria, Egypt, Cyrene, Epirus and Macedonia. He also sent missionaries to the south as far as Ceylon (Sri Lanka). Within his own empire also, he sent missionaries to various parts of the country. The names of some of the missionaries and the countries to which they were assigned as recorded in the Mahavamsa are:

"Majjhantika to Kashmir and Gandhara; Mahadeva to Mahisamandala (Mysore); Rakkhita to Vanavasi (North Kanara in Karnataka); Yona Dhammarakhita to Apparantaka; Mahadhammarakhita to Maharashtra; Maharakkhita to Yonaloka (Greek settlements of North-West India); Majjhima to Himavanta (Himalayan region); Sona and Uttara to Suvarnabhumi (Burma); and Mahinda, Itthiya, Uttiya, Sambhala and Bhadasara to Sri Lanka".

The two missionaries deputed by Asoka to the Andhra-Karnataka region, which formed part of the Mauryan empire, were stationed at Mahisamandala (Mysore) and Vanavasi (North Kanara) in Karnataka. Though the names of the southern kingdoms of the Pandya, Cholas, and Cheras are not specifically mentioned in the Mahavamsa yet it is not unreasonable to assume that Mahadeva and Rakkhita or some other monks must have preached the *Dhamma* in these kingdoms as well. "It was by Buddhist missions", observes Mr. Barth that "the powerful Emperor came into relation with the kings of Dekhan, over whom he appears to have exercised a kind of protectorate[13]".

Turning to the physical location of the edicts of Asoka, we find that no Asokan Pillars have so far been discovered in South India but the share of South India in the case of Rock Edicts is quite substantial. The major rock edicts of Asoka comprising a set of 14 edicts have been discovered at six places in modern India. One of them is at Yerragudi in Andhra Pradesh; the other five being at Girnar in Gujarat, Sopara in Maharashtra, Dhauli and Jaugada in Orissa, and Kalsi in Uttar Pradesh.

Briefly, the 14 edicts found at Yerragudi in district Kurnool of Andhra Pradesh cover the following topics:

I. Prohibition of animal sacrifice for religious purposes and prohibition of *Samaja* festive gatherings.

II. Provision of medical treatment, shade and water for men and animals throughout his dominion and also in the neighbouring countries.

III. Institution of quinquennial tours of officials for the propagation of *Dhamma* instruction.

IV. Success attained by his propagation of the *Dhamma* is greater than that attained by conventional methods.

V. Appointment of the *Dhamma-Mahamatras*, and their activities.

VI. Asoka's tireless zeal in serving the interest of the public.

VII. Asoka's impartiality towards all religious sects.

VIII. Commencement of the *Dhamma-tours*.

IX. Futility of conventional auspicious ceremonies, and the superior merits of *Dhamma-practices*.

X. The object of Asoka's exertions.

XI. Superiority of the gifts of *Dhamma*.

XII. The desirability of inter-communal understanding and regard.

XIII. The evils of conquest by war and the excellence of conquest by *Dhamma*.

XIV. A review of the Rock-Edicts.

As against one major rock edict of Asoka in South India, there are as many as eleven minor rock edicts in South India out of seventeen in the whole of India. The minor rock edicts of Asoka in South India are in Andhra (2) and Karnataka (9). In Andhra Pradesh, the minor rock edicts are at at Yerragudi and Rajula-Mandagiri in district Kurnool. In Karnataka, these are at Maski, Gavimath, Palkigundu and Koppal in Raichur district; Brahmagiri, Siddhapura and Jaitingarameshwara in Chitradurg district; and Nittur and Udegolam in Bellary district. The subject matter of both the minor rock edicts deals with "the fruit of zeal in practising Dhamma". In some cases, the version slightly differs. Here, we reproduce the Maski text of Edict I, the Brahmagiri text and Yerragudi text of Edict II:

Edict I - Maski Text[14]

This is a proclamation of Asoka, Beloved of the Gods.

It is now more than two years and a half that I am a lay follower of the Buddha. It is again more than a year now that I am devoutly attached to the *Sangha* and devoted to exertion for the sake of *Dhamma*. In Jambudvipa, the gods, who were formerly unmingled with men, have now become mingled with them.

This object, gained by me, can be achieved even by a poor man if he is devoted to *Dhamma*. One should not consider that the rich alone can achieve this object. The poor and the rich should both be told: If you act in this manner, this laudable achievement will last for a long time and thus increase to one and a half times".

Edict II - Brahmagiri Text[15]

Thus saith the Beloved of the Gods with reference to the above.

One should obey one's mother and father and likewise one's elders. One should be steadfast in one's kindness towards living beings. One should speak the truth. In this way, one should propound these attributes of *Dhamma*.

In the same way, the pupil should honour his teacher and this practice should be established by one in the proper manner among one's relations. This is an ancient rule and the principle is longstanding. One should act in this way.

Edict II - Yerragudi Text[16]

Thus saith the Beloved of the Gods.

You should act as instructed by the Beloved of the Gods. You should order the Rajjukas and the Rajjukas in their turn shall order the people of the countryside as well as the local officers called Rashtrika in the following words: 'Mother and father are to be obeyed. And similarly elders are to be obeyed. Living beings should be treated with kindness. Truth must be spoken. These attributes of *Dhamma* are to be propounded.' Thus you should order in the words of the Beloved of the Gods".

In the light of the foregoing evidence, it can be safely assumed that Buddhism had taken roots in South India in the third century BC. How the seeds of *Dhamma* planted by Asoka flowered in South India in the following centuries will be discussed in the subsequent chapters.

Notes and References

1. K.V. Ramesh, The Asokan Inscription At Sannathi, the Indian Historical Review. July 1987 & January 1988, Vol. XIV, Nos. 1-2, Indian Council of Historical Research, New Delhi, pp. 36-42.
2. The Hindustan Times, New Delhi, 20 March, 1989.
3. Samuel Beal, Buddhist Records of the Western World - translated from the Chinese of Hiuen Tsang, Delhi Reprint, 1981, Vol. II, p. 230.
4. South India Inscriptions, Volume I, pp. 144-145.
5. Cambridge History of India, P. 499.
6. A History of South India, Madras, 1984 edition, p. 85.
7. R. Sathianata Aiyer, Studies in the Ancient History of Tondaimandalam, Madras, 1944. Cf. Political and Cultural History of India, Volume I, S. Natarajan and Mrs. Prema Ramakrishna, Fifth edition, Hyderabad, 1983, pp. 290-91.
8. Romila Thapar, Asoka and the Decline of the Mauryas, Delhi, 1973, p. 251.
9. Dr. R. Nagaswamy, Asoka and the Tamil Country : A New Link, in The Sunday Express, Masgazine Section, Madras, 6 December, 1981.
10. D.C. Sircar, Inscriptions of Asoka, Delhi, 1956, p. 43.
11. Ibid., p. 54.
12. Romila Thapar, Asoka and the Decline of the Mauryas, p. 256.
13. Cf. K.P. Padmanabha Menon, History of Kerala, Vol. I, New Delhi, 1982 edition, p. 462.
14. Sircar, Inscriptions of Asoka, pp. 34-35.
15. Ibid., p. 36.
16. Ibid., p. 37.

4

Andhra Pradesh

The Telugu speaking Andhra State was formed in 1953 after it was separated from the former State of Madras in the wake of a violent agitation. This Caesarian birth of the Andhra State led to the appointment of the States Reorganisation Commission. Based on the recommendations of this Commission, the Telengana region of the former princely State of Hyderabad was merged with the Andhra State to form the present Andhra Pradesh, with Hyderabad as its capital, in 1956. In area, Andhra Pradesh is 2, 76, 814 square kilometres.

(I) ROYAL PATRONAGE

As the story of Bavari and his sixteen disciples given in the *Sutta-Nipata*, an oldest Pali text, and narrated by us in Chapter II, reveals, the gospel of the Buddha had reached Andhra during the life-time of the Blessed One. And when Andhra came under the suzernity of Asoka (BC 273-BC 232), Buddhism got a further fillip. The first and foremost Buddhist shrine in Andhra, the *Mahachaitya* at Amaravati, in distinct Guntur, is said to have been founded by Mahadeva, a monk-missionery, deputed by Asoka to preach and propagate the *Dhamma* in the Andhra-Karnataka region. A fragmentary inscription[1] on a sandstone slab, apparently cut from an Asokan pillar, discovered at Amaravati gives credence to this view. The discovery of three Asokan rock edicts - one major and one minor at Yerragudi, and one minor edict at Rajula-Mandagiri in Kurnool district further fortify this assumption. Asoka also mentions Andhra, alongwith other imperial territories, in the thirteenth major rock edict (Shahbazgarhi version) which tells us how the people in the Mauryan empire responded to Asoka's *Dhamma-campaign*. The edict says[2] : "Likewise here in the imperial territories among the Greeks, Kambojas, Nabhakas and Nabhapanktis, Bhojas and Pitinikas, Andhras and Parindas (Pulindas), everywhere the people follow the Beloved of the God's instructions in *Dhamma*. Even where the envoys of the Beloved of the Gods have not gone, people hear of his conduct according to *Dhamma*, his precepts and his instructions in *Dhamma*, and they follow *Dhamma* and will continue to follow it".

Asoka's *Dhamma-Vijaya* campaign was quite successful in Andhra-desa. Following the lead given by the Mauryan Emperor, the local kings of Andhra also patronised Buddhism. The two inscriptions of probably second century BC discovered from the Buddhist *stupa* at Bhattiprolu in district Guntur mention the name of a king Kubarika, a local Buddhist ruler.[3]

When the Mauryan Empire disintegrated, the Satavahanas came to power in the Deccan. The Satavahana dynasty was founded by Simukha who ruled from BC 230-BC 212. Simukha was succeeded by his younger brother Kanha or Krishna. The Satavahanas had sway over Andhra, Maharashtra and even a part of Karnataka. They ruled for about 450 years except for a brief interlude when they were ousted by the Saka Satrap, Nahapana from the Nasik-Karle region of Maharashtra. Gautamiputra Satakarni, the twenty-third king, who ruled from AD 106-130 was the greatest Satavahana king. During his reign, the Satavahana empire reached its climax. He re-conquered the Nasik-Karla region and brought back the lost glory to the Satavahana empire. Gautamiputra Satakarni was succeeded by his son, Vasisthiputra Pulumavi who ruled from AD 130 to 150. The last powerful Satavahana king was Yajnasri Satakarni who ruled from AD 166-196.

A number of inscriptions of the Satavahana kings found in the Buddhist caves at Nasik in Maharashtra indicate that from the very beginning the Satavahanas had patronised Buddhism. The first Satavahana inscription in the Nasik Caves is that of king Kanha or Krishna who ruled in the second century BC. The inscription clearly says[4], "under king Krishna of the Satavahana family this cave has been caused to be made by the officer-in-charge of the *Sramanas* at Nasik. "Later, the Nasik-Karle region was conquered by the Kshatratas, under the leadership of Nahapana, in the first century AD. The Nasik-Karle region was reconquered by the 23rd Satavahana king, Gautamiputra Siri Satakarni sometime during AD 106 - 130. Queen Gotami Balasiri, mother of the king, in grateful thanks to the Buddha, showered gifts on the Buddhist community at Nasik. The inscriptions in Cave III of Gautamiputra Satakarni, his mother, Queen Balasiri and of his son, Vasisthiputra Siri Pulumavi, give ample evidence of the royal support to Buddhism.

An inscription dated in the regnal year 24 of Gautamiputra Satakarni states that "king Gautamiputra Satakarni and Mahadevi Jivasuta Rajamata, the great queen, the king's mother, `whose son is alive' made a grant in the Govardhana district (Nasik) in favour of certain Buddhist monks dwelling in the caves[5]." The inscription further refers to `making over a second field in place of the first which had gone out of cultivation'. Another inscription refers to granting of a field previously `enjoyed by Usavadata' to the monks. The third inscription in the same cave is by Vasisthiputra Pulumavi (AD 130-159) in honour of his father (Gautamiputra Satakarni) and grand mother (Balasiri). According to this inscription[6], `Gautamiputra Satakarni, who raised his family to high fortune, as a pious gift, built a cave on the top of Tiranhu mountain and the king's mother Mahadevi Gotami Balasiri gave it to the monks of the Bhadrayaniya sect'. Yet another inscription by Vasisthiputra Pulumavi speaks about the granting of a village by the king for the support of the Bhadrayaniya monks of Nasik Caves. The inscription ends with the words, "Vinhnupala proclaims the praise of the Lord.

Obeisance to the Being exalted in perfection and majesty the excellent Jina, the Buddha."

There are also two inscriptions[7] by the Satavahana kings in the Karle or Karla Buddhist Caves in Maharashtra. The first inscription records the gift of the village Karajaka by Gautamiputra Satakarni to the monks of Valuraka (Verul) caves for the support of the Mahasanghika. The second inscription of the time of Vasisthiputra Pulumavi records the gift of a nine-celled hall to the Mahasanghikas.

The inscriptions of the last powerful Statavhana king, Yajnasri Satakarni (AD 166-196) are also available at Nasik in Cave XV. An inscription states[8] : "Success! on the first day of third-3rd fortnight of winter, in the seventh-7th - year of the king, the Lord Sriyajna Satakarni, son of Gotami, the Mahasenapatni Vasu, wife of the Mahasenapati Bhavagopa, of the Kausiki family, has completed and given, as an abode of the Universal *Sangha* of monks, this cave which had been excavated for many years, but, after having been created by the ascetic Bopaki, had remained uncompleted".

As noticed earlier, the Nasik-Karla region was conquered by the Kshatratas in the first century AD. The Kshatratas too patronised the Buddhist community at Nasik. In fact, Usavadata, son of Dinika, and son-in-law of Mahakshatrapa Nahapana, who became governor of Nasik during this period proved to be a great benefactor of the Buddhist monks at Nasik. A number of inscriptions by him in Cave VIII at Nasik tell us about the excavation of new caves as well as gifts made by him and his family to the Bhikkhu *Sangha*. In all, Cave VIII has as many as six inscriptions referring to Nahapana.

During the reign of the latter Satavahana Kings, who made Dhanyakataka, in district Guntur of Andhra Pradesh, their royal seat, the Amaravati *Stupa* (Maha-chaitya) was enlarged and also surrounded by a new highly ornamental railing carved with beautiful reliefs and elegant designs. The three inscriptions discovered at Amaravati of the second century AD refer to three

Satavahana Kings: Vasishthiputra Pulumavi (AD 130-159), Sivamaka Sada or Siva Sri (AD 159-166), and Yajnasri Satakarni (AD 166-196). Yajnasri Satakarni was the last important King of the Satavahana dynasty. He was patron and friend of the famous Buddhist saint and scholar, Nagarjuna, the founder of the Madhyamika school of Buddhist philosophy. He is said to have built a monastery for Nagarjuna at Sri-parvata, where the Acharya lived towards the evening of his life. The close association of Yajansri Satakarni with Nagarjuna is confirmed by the "Suhrllekha or Letter to a Friend" which Nagarjuna wrote as a letter of moral and spiritual exhortation to the Satavahana King. The patronage of Buddhism by the Satavahana royal house is further confirmed by a four-line Prakrit inscription on a pillar at Nagarjunakonda of the sixth regnal year of Vijaya Satakarni who succeeded Yajnasri Satakarni in AD 196 or AD 203 as some scholars opine.

After the decline of the Satavahanas, the Ikshvakus came to power in Andhra. The Ikshvakus made Sri-parvata or Nagarjunakonda their capital. Chamtasri, sister of the founder of this royal house, Vasisthiputra Siri Chamtamula, was an ardent devotee of the Buddha. As a result of the patronage of this pious lady and other Ikshvaku queens and princesses, the valley of Nagarjunakonda became a flourishing Buddhist centre in the third century AD. As at Amaravati, so also at Nagarjunakonda the inscriptions are in Brahmi script, and open with the words '*Sidham*' i.e. 'Success' or 'Let there be success'. Some of the inscriptions glorify the Buddha in these words:

"Sidham namo bhagavato devaraja sakatasa supabudhabudhino savamnuno sava-sat-anukampakasa...."

"Success! Adoration to the Lord, the Supreme Buddha, honoured by the Lord of the gods, enlightened with perfect enlightenment, omniscient, compassionate towards all sentient beings".

The largest number of inscriptions at Nagarjunakonda pertain to the reign of the second Ikshvaku king, Sir Virapurushadatta or Virapurisadata who is said to have embraced Buddhism. The king claims to be belonging to the same clan as the Lord Buddha, and took keen interest in the progress of Buddhism. With his blessings, the royal ladies gave liberal donations to the Buddhist monks and monasteries. The eight royal inscriptions found at the Ayaka Pillars B2, B4, B5, C2, C3, C4, C5 and the First Apsidal temple at Nagarjunakonda of the reign of Virapurushadatta are reproduced below in the same order:

"Success! The Mahatalavari Adavichatisiri (who is) the daughter of the Maharaja Vasithiputa Ikhaku Siri Chamtamula, the offerer of Asvamedha, the giver of many crores of gold, hundred thousands of kine and hundred thousands of ploughs (of land), of unimpeded purpose in all (his aims); (who is) the sister of King Siri Virapurisadata (and who is) the wife of the Mahasenapati, the Mahatalavara the Mahadandanayaka Khamdavisakhamnaka (of the family) of the Dhanakas, having due regard for both the houses to which she belongs and for the attainment by herself and happiness in both the worlds, has erected this pillar at the Mahachetiya of the Lord, the Supreme Buddha who is absorbed by the best of elements (i.e. by *Nirvana*). In the sixth year of (the reign of) king Siri Virapurisadata".[9] (B2).

"Success! Adoration to the Lord, the Supreme Buddha, honoured by the Lord of the gods, enlightened with prefect enlightenment omniscient, compassionate towards all sentient beings, freed from lust, hatred and delusion conquered by him the bull and musk-elephant among great spiritual leaders, absorbed by the best of elements (i.e. *Nirvana*). At the Mahachetiya, the Mahasenapatini Chulachatasirinika (who is) a daughter of (the family of) the Kulahakas and the wife of the Mahasenapati, the Mahatalavara, Vasithiputa Khamdachalikiremmanaka of (the family of) of Hiramnakas, for the attainment by herself of welfare and happiness in both the worlds and of *Nirvana* has created this stone pillar. In the sixth year of (the reign of) king Siri Virapurisadatta....[10]" (B4).

"Success! Adoration to the Lord, the Supreme Buddha, honoured by the Lord of the gods, enlightened with perfect enlightenment, ominiscient, compassionate towards all sentient beings, freed from lust, hatred and delusion conquered by him, the bull and musk-elephant among great spiritual leaders absorbed by the best of elements (i.e. *Nirvana*). At the Mahachetiya the Mahadevi Rudradharabhatarika, a Maharaja's daughter from Ujjeni (skt. Ujjaini) has erected this stone pillar for the attainment by herself of welfare and happiness and *Nirvana*. And while the Mahachetiya of this Great Vihara was being raised by the ladies, the Mahatalavaras, Chamitisirinika of (the family of) the Pukiyas one hundred and seventy (100+70) dinari-masakas and a pillar have been raised by the Mahatalavari. In the sixth year of (the reign of) king Siri Virapurisadatta[11] .." (B5).

"Success! Adoration to the Lord, the supreme Buddha honoured by the Lord of the gods, absorbed by the best of elements. At the Mahachetiya the Mahadevi Bapasirinika (who is) the daughter of Hammasirinika, the uterine sister of Maharaja Vasisthiputra Ikhaku Siri-Chatamula and (who is) the wife of king Siri Virapurisadata, with due regard for his mother Hammasirinika, and for the sake of attainment by herself of the bliss of *Nirvana* has erected this stone pillar. For the benefit of the Masters of the Aparamahavinaseliya sect has this pious foundation of the Mahachetiya been accepted. This pious foundation, consisting of the Mahachetiya, has been completed and the pillars have been set up by the Reverned Ananda, who knows the *Digha* and the *Majjhima* (nikayas) by heart, (who is) a disciple of the Masters of the *Arya-samgho* who are resident in Pamnagama and who are preachers and preceptors of the *Digha* and *Majjhima* (nikayas) and of the five Matukas. In the sixth year of (the reign of) king Siri Virapuribadata[12] ....." (C2).

"Success! Adoration to the Lord, the Supreme Buddha, honoured by the Lord of the gods, omniscient, compassionate towards all the sentient beings, freed from lust, hatred and delusion which have been conquered by him the bull and musk-elephant among great spiritual leaders, the perfectly Enlightened One, who is absorbed by the best of elements (i.e. by *Nirvana*). At the Mahachetiya, the Mahatalavari Cha(m) tisiri (who is) the uterine sister of Maharaja Vasisthiputra Ikhaku Siri Cha(m) tamula-absorbed by Mahasena the Lord of Virupakhas, the giver of crores of gold, hundred thousands of kine, and hundred thousands of ploughs (of land), unimpeded of purpose in all (his) aims, (She who is) the paternal aunt of king Madhariputa Siri Virapurisadata, (She who is) the wife of the Mahasenapati, the Mahatalavara, Vasithiputa Kamdasiri of (the family of) the Pukiyas; and the mother of Kamdasagaramnaka, she who, out of compassion for Sramanas, Brahmins, and those that are miserable, poor and destitute, is wont to bestow on them a matchless flow and ceaseless flow of Velamic gifts, she the great mistress of munificience devoted to all the virtuous, having due regard for the past, future and present (members) of both the houses to which she belongs for the attainment of welfare and happiness in both the worlds and in order to attain herself the bliss of Nirvana and for the attainment of welfare and happiness by all the world, has erected this pillar. In the sixth year of the reign of king Siri Virapurisadata[13] ..." (C3).

"Success! Adoration to the Lord, the Supreme Buddha, honoured by the Lord of the gods, absorbed by the best of elements. At the Mahachetiya the Mahadevi Chhathisiri (Skt. Shashthi-sri) (who is) the daughter of Hammasiri the uterine sister of Maharaja Vasithiputra Ikhaku Siri-Chamtamula-absorbed by Mahasena the Lord of Virupakhas, the giver of crores of gold, hundred thousands of kine and hundred thousands of ploughs (of land), unimpeded of purpose in all (his) aims, (she who is) the paternal aunt of king Madhariputa Siri Virapurisadata and (she who is) the wife of Maharaja Madhariputa Siri Virapurisadata, with due regard for her mother Hammasirinika and for the sake of attainment by herself of the bliss of *Nirvana*, has erected this pillar. In the sixth year of (the reign of) king Siri Virapurisadata[14] ....." (C4).

"Success! Adoration to the Lord, the supreme Buddha, absorbed by the best of elements. At the Mahachetiya the Mahatalavari (who is) the wife of the Mahasenapati, the Mahatalavara Vasithiputa Mahakamdasiri of (the family of) the

Pukiyas and (who is) the mother of the Mahasenapati, the Mahatalavara Vinhusiri (Skt. Vishnusri), with due regard to both the families to which she belongs, and for the sake of her own welfare and happiness in both the worlds and *Nirvana*, has erected this stone pillar. In the sixth year of (the reign of) Maharaja Siri-Virapurisadata[15] ....." (C5).

"Success! Adoration to the Lord Buddha. A chetiya-ghara (chaitya-hall) chatisiri (who is) the uterine sister of Maharaja Vasethiputa Siri-Chatamula of the house of Ikhaku, who is favoured (absorbed) by Mahasena, the Lord of Virupakhas, the giver of many crores of gold, hundred thousands of kine and hundred thousands of ploughs (of land) and who is of unimpeded purpose in all (his aims, (who is) the wife of Vasethiputa Khamdasiri of (the family of) the Pukiyas and (who is) the mother of Khamdasagaramnaga, for the longevity and for the victory of her son-in-law, king Madhariputa Siri Virapurisadata of the house of Ikhaku and for the attainment by herself of welfare and happiness in both the worlds and of *Nirvana*, having due regard to the past, future and present bliss of the great community of Buddhist monks consisting of all the holy men who have renounced the world and who have penetrated into various countries, and of both the houses to which she herself belongs, has erected a stone shrine surrounded by a cloister and provided with everything at the foot of the Mahachetiya for the benefit of the Masters, belonging to the sect of the Aparamahavinaseliyas. In the eighteenth year 18, of king Siri Virapurisadata[16] ....." (Apsidal temple).

Siri Virapurushadatta's son and successor, Ehuvula or Chatamula II was also a Buddhist. Like his father, he ruled for 24 years. His reign marked the golden period of Nagarjunakonda as it was during his reign that the construction of Buddhist shrines reached its peak. Of the inscriptions of his reign, four royal inscriptions found on the *Ayaka* pillars are as follows:

"Success! Adoration to the Lord Buddha. This pious gift, a monastery provided with every thing has been erected for the benefit of the Masters belonging to the Bahusu (t)iya sect by

Mahadevi (Bhatideva), (who is) the daughter-in-law of Maharaja Vasi(t)-thiputta Siri Chamtamula of (the house of) the Ikhakus, who is favoured by Mahasena, the Lord of Virupakkhas, the giver of many crores of gold, hundred thousands of kine and hundred thousands of ploughs (of land) and who is of unimpeded purpose in all (his) aims, (and who is) the wife of Maharaja Siri-Ehuvula-Siri-Virapurisadatta. In the second year of (the reign of) Raja Vasi(t) thiputta Siri Ehuvula Chatamula of (the house of) the Ikhakus, the sixth-6-fortnight of summer, the tenth-10-day[17]."

"Success! Adoration to the Lord Buddha. This pious gift,the queen's monastery provided with everything has been erected for the benefit of the Masters belonging to the Bahusutiya sect by Mahadevi Bhatideva (who is) the daughter-in-law of Maharaja Vasethiput(t) a Siri Chamtamula, of (the house of) the Ikkhakus, who is favoured by Mahasena, the Lord of Virupakkhas, the giver of many crores of gold, hundred thousands of kine, and hundred thousands of ploughs (of land) and who is of unimpeded purpose in all (his) aims, (and who is) the wife of Maharaja Madhariput(t)a Siri-Virapurisadat(t)a of (the house of) the I(k)khakus. In the second year of the (the reign of) Raja Siri-Ehuvula Chatamula, the (sixth) fortnight of summer, the tenth day[18] ...."

"Success! Adoration to the Lord, the leader of the Law of the three worlds.... Mahadevi Bhatideva (who is) the daughter-in-law of Maharaja Vasethiputa Siri-Chatamula, of (the house of) the Ikkhakus, who is favoured by Mahasena, the lord of Virupakkhas, the giver of many crores of gold, hundred thousands of kine and hundred thousands of plough (of land) and who is of unimpeded purpose in all (his) aims, (and who is) the wife of Maharaja Madhariputa Siri-Virapurisadata of the house of the Ikkhakus; (and who is) the mother of Maharaja Siri-Ehuvula-Chatamula has erected... this monastery provided with all essentials for the Masters of the Bahusutiya sect[19]."

"Success! Adoration to the Lord, the Supreme Buddha. In the eleventh year of (the reign of) Maharaja Vasethiputa Siri-Ehuvula

(Chata) mula of (the house of) the Ikkhakus, the first (fortnight of) the seventh day. Mahadevi (ko) da(ba)lisiri (who is) the grand-daughter of Maharaja Vasethiputa, Siri-Chatamula of (the house of) the Ikkhakus; (who is) the sister of Maharaja Vasethiputa Siri-Ehuvala-Chatamula of (the house of) the Ikkhakus; and (who is) the wife of the Maharaja of Vanavasaka has erected this pillar and monastery for the benefit of the Masters of the Mahi(sa) saka sect, on behalf of the community of the Four Quarters, and for the sake of welfare and happiness of all sentient beings. (It has been) carried out by the Master, the great preacher of the Law, the Thera Dhammaghosa[20]."

The construction of Buddhist shrines at Nagarjunakonda came to an end in the eleventh regnal year of Rudrapurusha, the last known Ikshvaku King. In all, more than thirty shrines came up in the Nagarjunakonda Valley during the Ikshvaku rule. Nagarjunakonda was, therefore, the largest and most important Buddhist settlement in South India in the third century AD. The Ikshvaku Kings also extended their patronage to the Buddhist shrines at other places, such as Amaravati and Jaggayyapeta.

Besides the Ikshvakus, the Bodhi dynasty[21], which ruled over some parts of North-western Deccan, in the third century AD, was another royal Buddhist family. Some of their coins have 'Bodhi tree' within a railing. From this, it is surmised that they derived their surname from the Bodhi Tree under which the Buddha had attained enlightenment. The names of the kings of the Bodhi dynasty as recorded in the coins are : Sribodhi, Sivabodhi, Chandrabodhi and Virabodhi.

About the middle of the fourth century AD, there flourished in Andhra, Damodravarman, a king of the Ananda or Andhra dynasty. He too was a Buddhist and built many buildings for the *Sangha*. In the plates of Damodravarman discovered in the village of Mattepad in the Ongole taluk of Guntur district, the king is referred to as 'Maharaja-Sri Damodaravarmano' or 'the glorious Maharaja Damodaravarman[22]'. The Mattepad Plates further mention that 'he meditates on the feet of the Blessed

Samyak Sambuddha' (*bhavatah samyakasambuddhasya padanudhyata*). Such a devout king naturally built many Buddhist shrines in Andhra. One of the *Chaityas* constructed by him has been identified by the scholars with the *Kopetesvara* temple at Chezarla in district Guntur to which usage it seems to have been converted by the Hindus when Buddhism fell from its place of privilege.

(II) SAINTS AND SCHOLARS

Within 100 years of the Mahaparinirvana of the Buddha differences arose among the Buddhist monks as to the correct interpretation of the monastic discipline and teachings of the Master. It is said that the monks of the Vajji country had started practising the Ten Points[23] (*dasa vathani*) which were regarded as unorthodox indulgence by the western monks led by Yasa. To settle this dispute a *Sangiti* (Council) was convened at Vaisali. Seven hundred monks participated in this Council. In an unanimous verdict, the Council, which was presided over by Ven. Sabbakami, declared the conduct of the Vajji monks unlawful. The Vajji monks, however, refused to accept the verdict. This resulted in a schism in the *Sangha*. The defiant Vajji monks later came to be known as Mahasanghikas.

The first schism was followed by a series of schisms leading to the formation of different sub-sects, and in the following centuries, there emerged as many as eighteen sub-sects, that is, seven sub-sects of the Mahasanghikas and eleven sub-sects of the Theravadins, each with its own interpretations of the canonical teachings.

The Mahasanghikas migrated from Magadha into two streams, one went towards the north and the other towards the south. Those who migrated to the south, settled down in the Andhradesa around Amaravati and Dhanyakataka. Later, their sub-sects[24] set up their centres on the hills around Nagarjunakonda. These sub-sects, which collectively came to be known as the Andhakas[25] , were the Pubbaseliyas or

Uttaraseliyas, Aparaseliyas, Siddhatthikas, Rajagirikas, and Caityikas. The Caityikas were so known because they attached great importance to the worship of the stupa or chaitya. Amaravati was their main centre, and significantly enough, in some inscriptions discovered at Amaravati, the great stupa is called *"Cetikyanam machacetiyasa"*, i.e. the great chaitya of the Chaityakas.[26]

The Mahasanghikas, in particular their sub-sects in Andhra, introduced new concepts like the one that the Buddhas were *lokottara* (supermundane) and were free from impurities. The *lokuttara* (super-human) conception of the Buddha led to the origin and development of the *Trikaya* doctrine or the three bodies of the Buddha - the *dharmakaya*, the body representing the cosmic principle; the *sambhogkaya*, the body representing the divine principle; and the *rupakaya*, the body representing the human incarnation. This paved way for the emergence of the Mahayana Buddhism in about the first century AD.

Nagarjuna was one of the greatest Mahayana teachers. He propounded the Madhyamika school of philosophy, also known as Sunyavada. Waters described Nagarjuna as "one of the wonders and mysteries of latter Buddhism[27] ", and Valles Poussin calls him "mysterious and miraculous person[28] ".

As in the case of many other Buddhist savants, mystery surrounds the life of Nagarjuna. It is, however, generally agreed that he was born in South India in the second century AD, and was a friend and contemporary of the Satavahana King, Yajnasri Satakarni (166-196 AD). According to another tradition, Nagarjuna was a native of South Kosala or modern Vidarbha.

According to the biography of Nagarjuna translated into Chinese in about AD 405 by Kumarajiva, Nagarjuna on joining the Buddhist Order studied the Buddhist texts available to him and grasped their meaning in only 90 days; and not being satisfied with them, he wandered in search of other texts. Consequently, he received the Mahayana sutra, *Prajnaparamitasutra*, from an old monk in the Himalayan region[29] ; and also procured a commentary on it with the help of a Nagaraja (Naga chief) who led him into the sea and opened up for him the "Treasury of the Seven Jewels" (*Saptaratnakosa*)[30] ". Whatever may be the truth in this legend, the Mahayana sutra, *Prajnaparamita*, became popular only after Nagarjuna propagated its teachings.

A large number of works are attributed to Nagarjuna, who was doubtless a versatile genious and philosopher. Among his authentic works in Sanskrit, the most important and the monumental one is the *Madhyamaksasastra* (*Madhyamika-karika*) in which Nagarjuna makes a critical examination of other Buddhist schools, especially the **Sarvastivada** view point. This work "written in a supremely forceful and elegant style, consists of 400 verses (karikas) distributed over 27 chapters, each of which is devoted to the examination of a particular topic".

The Madhyamika school derives its name from the middle path it advocates, that is, the non-acceptance of the two views concerning existence and non-existence, eternity and non-eternity, self and non-self and so on. In short, it advocates neither the theory of reality nor that of the unreality of the world, but merely of relativity[31] ." In the *Madhyamika-Karika*, Nagarjuna presents in a systematic manner the philosophy of the Madhyamika school. It teaches that *sunyata* (the indescribable absolute) is the absolute. There is no difference between *samsara* (phenomenal world) and *nirvana* or *sunyata* reality)". In other words, the Madhyamikas believe that "all things are of a non-essential and indefinable character, and void at bottom". Since the Madhyamika school holds *sunyata* to be the central idea of its philosophy, it is called *Sunyavada* also.

The *Pratityasamputpada-hrdya-sastra* (Secret of the Casually Dependent Origination) gives an exposition of the twelve linked chain of the course of phenomenal existence. The *Yuktisastika* (Sixty Arguments) and *Sunyata-saptati* (Seventy verses on Unreality) are short compediums on the basic tenets of Mahayana. The *Mahaprajnaparamitasastra* is a voluminous commentary on the Large '*Prajnaparamita*'. Another important commentary written by Nagarjuna is *Dasabhumi-vibhasa-sastra*. The *Bhavasankrantisastra* is another notable commentary. Nagarjuna also wrote devotional verses, *Catuh-stava*, a kind of hymn in four parts, Lastly, the "*Suhrllekha* or Letter to a Friend" which he wrote as a letter of moral and spiritual exhortation to his friend, the Satavahana King.

Other works of Nagarjuna are : Vigrahavyavartani, Dvasdas-mukha-sastra, Ekasloka-sastra, Vaidlaya-Sutra, Prakarana, Mahayana-vismika, Bodhicitta-vivarna and Ratnavli.

The *Madhyamika Karika* of Nagarjuna, being the basic text of Madhyamika school of thought has been a subject of comment for centuries. There are as many as seven commentaries by eminent acharyas, besides the "*Akutobhaya* (The Safe One) said to be an auto comment by Nagarjuna. The best known commentary is that of Chandrakirti, the *Prasannapada* or "Clear Worded". This commentary still survives in Sanskrit: the others being available only in Tibetan or Chinese translations. In the Chinese collection, three available commentaries are: (i) *Prajnamula* of Pingala, (ii) *Prajnapradipa* of Bhavaviveka, and (iii) *Mahayana madhyamakadarsana-vyakhya-sastra* of Sthiramati. Those available in the Tibetan Collection are: Bhavaviveka's *Prajnapradipa*, Buddhapalita's *Vritti* and Chandrakirti's *Prasannapada*.

Nagarjuna's letter to the Satavahana King, "*Suhrllekha*" has also been a popular text with the Chinese and Tibetan scholars. It was translated into Chinese three times-by Gunavarman, and Sanghavarman in the fifth century AD, and by I-tsing in the seventh century AD. *Suhrllekha* was translated into Tibetan by Sarvajnadeva. The Tibetan Collection also has four commentaries[32] on *Suhrllekha*. Of these, the best one is by Mi-pham written in the nineteenth century. In India, *Suhrllekha* was a popular religious book for centuries. According to the Chinese pilgrim-scholar, I-tsing, who was in India in AD 673-685 Nagarjuna's *Suhrllekha* was so popular at the time of his visit that "children vied with each other in committing it to memory and the adults considered it their life long companion". The reason for *Suhrllekha's* popularity seems to be its emphasis on the observance of the path of piety as taught by the Buddha.

The mighty Nagarjuna lived a very long life.[33] He is said to have possessed some uncommon psychic powers and had prolonged his life through various expedients. Nagarjuna travelled all over India, and as a result of his towering personality Buddhism became quite popular. Though he was associated with Nalanda but he mainly lived at Amaravati and Sriparvata in Andhra. Towards the evening of his life he stayed at Sriparvata where the Satavahana King had built a monastery for him. Sriparvata (in Guntur distt.) was later named as Nagarjunakonda after his name.

After the advent of Nagarjuna, it was primarily the Madhyamika philosophy which travelled abroad and became the basis of Mahayana Buddhism there. Even today, it is so in the countries following the Mahayana tradition. In India, the impact of Nagarjuna was so great that "practically all the Brahminical schools found it necessary to adapt the dialectic of Nagarjuna to their own needs. Gaudapada and Sankara, as is well known, borrowed much of their method and many of their conclusions from the Madhyamikas. The Advaita system of Vedanta is in a sense a less rigorous and more compromising continuation of the Madhyamika teaching[34]".

Arya Deva, a Sinhalese by birth, was a worthy and immediate successor of Nagarjuna. Arya Deva is also known as Kanadeva, or "the one-eyed", and *Nilanetra,* or "the blue-eyed". It is said that learning the fame of Nagarjuna, he came from Sri Lanka and met Nagarjuna at Sriparvata. About their first meeting, the Tibetan tradition tells us that on reaching there, Arya Deva addressed the gate-keeper, saying; "Please be good enough to announce me". Accordingly, the gate-keeper informed Nagarjnuna of Arya Deva's arrival, Nagarjuna filled up his begging bowl with water and commanded his disciple and attendant to go and hold the water in front of Arya Deva.

The disciple held the begging-bowl as told and soon returned with perturbation to Nagarjuna. "What did the visitor say?" Nagarjuna asked. The disciple answered excitedly: He was silent and said nothing, he only dropped a needle into the water". Nagarjuna said: "He is a wise man. To know the springs of action, this is the privilege of a Deva, to penetrate subtle principles is the privilege of an Arya. Such full wisdom as this entitles him to be allowed to enter forthwith."

Thus gaining the confidence of Nagarjuna at the very first meeting, Arya Deva soon became his chief disciple. Like Nagarjuna, Arya Deva was also the author of a number of valuable works on the Madhyamika philosophy. The *Catuh Sataka,* a work of 400 Karikas, written by him is considered as one of the principle works of the Madhyamika school, besides Nagarjuna's Madhyamika-karika. In this work, Arya Deva while clarifying the meaning of Relativity, or Non-substantiality, has devoted even greater attention than Nagarjuna to refute the views of the Sankhya and Vaisesika systems of Brahaminical philosophy[35] ".

Arya Deva was a multi-faceted genius. It is said that Arya Deva was "a formidable debator and many times vanquished his opponents in the public discussions". Thus he had created many enemies. Enraged by the defeat of a Hindu scholar, inimical to Buddhism, one of his disciples attacked Arya Deva with a sword while he was engaged in meditation, as a result of which he died[36]. This event took place at Ranganatha, a suburb of Kanchipuram in Tamil Nadu, where Arya Deva had stayed for a number of years.

Of the large number of Buddhist monks who preached and propagated the *Dhamma* in Andhra in the early centuries of the Christian Era, a few names have survived in the inscriptions found at Amaravati and Nagarjunakonda. An inscription at Amaravati tells us that the renovation of the ornamental railing around the *Maha Chaitya* was supervised by a monk named Buddharakkhita. And the donors were: a nun, who was Ven.

Buddharakkhita's disciple, Likhita, a monk from Pataliputra in Bihar, three Tamil pilgrims, and the local Buddhists. Some other Buddhist monks mentioned in the Amaravati inscriptions are: Agnisri Chandra, Dhammarakkhita, Dhammasira, Pasama and Mahadhammakadhika.

The Nagarjunakonda inscriptions refer to one Ananda Thera who knew the *Digha* and *Majjhima Nikayas* by heart. It is also stated that Ananda Thera was a disciple of the Masters of the *Arya Sangha* who are resident in Pamagama. Another great preacher of the Law was Thera Dhammaghosha.

The fame of Nagarjunakonda attracted Buddhist saints and scholars from all parts of India, and even foreign lands, in particular from Sri Lanka. The foreign Bhikkhus had even specific *Viharas* for their use. For instance, the Chula-Dhammagiri *Vihara* was known as *Sihala Vihara* as it was primarily meant for the Sri Lankan monks. This *Vihara* was built by one devout Buddhist lady, Bodhisri of Gopagama during the reign of Vira-purushadatta, the famous Ikshvaku king. An inscription discovered on the floor of the *Chaitya* of this *Vihara* records that the devout Bodhisri had also made liberal donations to many other shrines at Nagarjunakonda, and that these works were supervised by three monks, namely, Thera Chandamukha, Thera Dhamnanandi and Thera Nagar. Beginning with the glorification of the Buddha, the inscription reads as follows[37]:

"Success! Adoration to the Lord Buddha, born of a race (which is) sprung from hundreds of sages and excellent kings of Ikshvaku's lineage; who has shown the road to welfare and happiness to gods and men and all beings, who has conquered and put down the pride and arrogance of Mara's hosts called lust, anger, fear, desire, thirst, delusion and hatred; who, great of power, is possessed of the ten powers, who has set in motion the Wheel of the Law (pertaining to) the Eight-fold Path, whose graceful and well formed feet (are marked with) the sign of the wheel, whose splendour is that of the newly risen sun, whose sight is lovely as that of autumnal moon, and who is magnified by the thoughts of all the world. In the fourteenth-14th-(year) of king Mathariputa, in the sixth-6th-fortnight of winter on the thirteenth-13th-day. For the benefit of the ..... masters and of the fraternities (of monks) of Tambapamna (Ceylon) who have converted Kashmir, Gandhara, China, Chilata. Tosali, Avaramta, Vanga, Vanavasi, Yavana, Damila, Palura and the Isle of Tambapamni (Ceylon). At Siriparvata on the east side of Vijayapuri at the convent on the Lesser Dhammagiri a Chaitya hall with a flooring of slabs, with a chaitya and provided with all the necessaries, was caused to be made by the female lay-member Bodhisiri for the sake of her own husband Budhimnaka, and of his father, the householder Revata residing at Govagama and of his mother Buddhamnika and his brother .... and of (his) sister ...... and of (his) brother's sons...... and of (his) sister's sons ...... and (for the sake) of her own grandfather ..... and of her maternal uncles .... and of her maternal grandmother ..... and of her own father .... and of her daughter ..... of her sons .... and of her daughter-in-law ..... And even thus wise a chaitya-hall at the Kulaha-*Vihara* a shrine for the Bodhi-tree at the Sihala-*Vihara* one-I-cell at the Great Dhammagiri, a mandava-pillar at the Mahavihara, a hall for religious practice at the Devagiri, a tank, verandah and mandava at Puvasela, a stone mandava at the eastern gate of the great chaitya at Kantakasela, three-3-cells at Hiramuthuva, seven-7-cells at Papila, a stone mandava at Puphagiri, a stone mandava at the vihara. And all this above described has been dedicated for the endless welfare and happiness of the assembly of saints and for that of the whole world. This work was caused to be made by the three superintendents of works, the thera Chamdamukha, and the thera Dhammanandi and the thera Naga. (It is) the work of the stone mason Vidhika."

Another undated Prakrit inscription on a foot-print slab records the installation of the Buddha-pada in the monastery of the Maha-viharavasins of the Theravada-Vibhajjavada School. It further records that the Theravadin teachers were experts in the nine-fold teaching of the Buddha and they preached the Dhamma in Kashmira, Gandhara, Yavana, Vanavasi and Tamrapani island (Sri Lanka). The text of this inscription is as follows[38]:

1. *Sidham achariyanam Theriyanam Vibhaja-vadanam Kasmira-Gandhara-Yavana-Vanavasa-Tambapamnidipa-pasadakanam.*
2. *Mahavihara-vasinam nava (m)ga-Sathu-sasana-etha-vyajana-vinichhya-visaradanam ariya-va (m) sa-pa-veni-dharanam.*
3. *vihara Bhagavato pada samghada nipatithapito sava-satanam hitasukh-athanava ti.*

Translation

Let there be success! The pair of feet of the Lord (i.e. the Buddha) has been installed, with the prayer for the welfare and happiness of all beings, in the monastery of the teachers who are Theriyas (i.e. There-vadins) (and) Vibhajja-vadas (i.e. Vibhajja-vadins), who caused delight to the people of Kashmira, Gandhara, Yavana, Vanavasa and Tamraparnidvipa; who are the residents of the Great Monastery; who are experts in the determination of the meaning and implication of the nine-fold teachings of the Buddha; (and) who know the traditions of the (four) classes of (Buddhist) teachers by heart."

(III) BUDDHIST SITES AND SHRINES

The popularity of Buddhism in Andhra was at its peak from the second century BC to fourth century AD, though it continued to be a living faith till atleast the ninth century AD. During the glorious epoch, the whole of Andhra was studded with Buddha Viharas. By now, more than 100 Buddhist settlements have been discovered in Andhra. The river Krishna, the life-line of Andhra, had a string of Buddhist shrines on its banks - Alluru, Amaravati, Bezwada, Ghantasala, Goli, Gummadidurru, Jaggayyapeta and Nagarjunakonda, The other notable Buddhist shrines in ancient Andhra were at Arugolanu, Bavikonda, Bhattiprolu, Ganjam, Gooty, Gudivada, Guntapalli, Kanuparti, Kodavli, Lingrajapalli, Nelakondapalli, Peda, Pedamadduru, Ramatirtham, Ramireddipalli and Sankaram.

Amaravati

The most sacred shrine in ancient Andhra was the *Maha-Chaitya* at Amaravati, 32 kilometres from Guntur, on the bank of river Krishna. It was also the longest living Buddhist shrine. In a way, the history of Amaravati is the history of Buddhism in Andhra. The Amaravati *Stupa* was first built in the third century BC by a missionary monk, Mahadeva, sent by Asoka to preach Buddhism in this part of the country. Initially, it was a modest *stupa* enclosed by a granite railing. A fragment of a polished pillar bearing an Asokan edict discovered here confirms its erection during the reign of Asoka. In the following two or three centuries, the granite rail was replaced by the limestone one and the gateways were also renovated. A large number of inscribed sculptured fragments of this period include a limestone stele of the second century BC depicting scenes of Vaisali, Sravasti and Kusinagara with appropriate labels.

The Satavahanas, who ruled Andhra, after Asoka, for a long period of over 450 years were also sympathetic towards the Buddhist cause. During the reign of the latter Satavahana Kings, who made the nearby Dhanyakataka their royal seat, the Amaravati *stupa* was enlarged in AD second century and also surrounded by a new highly ornamental railing, carved with beautiful reliefs and elegant designs.

Of the three inscriptions of the latter Satavahana period, the earliest one refers to the gift of the Wheel of Law (*Dharma-Chakra*) at the western gate of the *Maha-Chaitya* during the reign of Vasishthiputra Pulumavi (AD 130-159). The second one refers to the replacement or renovation of a part of the railing during the reign of Siri Sivamaka Sada, generally identified with Siva-Sri (AD 159-166). The third inscription belongs to the period of Gautamiputra Yajnasri Satakarni (AD 166-196), the last important King of the Satavahana dynasty. Yajnasri Satakarni was the patron and friend of Acharya Nagarjuna, the famous Buddhist saint and scholar. Taranatha, the Tibetan historian, says that the erection of the sculptured rail at Amaravati was organised by Nagarjuna. According to an inscription, renovation of the railing was supervised by a monk, named Buddharakkhita. Apparently, this was at the instance of Acharya Nagarjuna. The donors included, a nun, who was Buddharakkhita's disciple, Likkhita, a monk from Pataliputra; three Tamil pilgrims; the people of **Dhanyakataka**; and a family from Ghantasala in Andhra.

The Amaravati *Stupa* in its final shape had "the vestiges of characteristic ayaka-platforms projecting out of the drum at cardinal directions. These platforms carried originally five ayaka-pillars, representing symbolically the five important events of Buddha's life: Birth, Renunciation, Enlightenment, First Sermon and *Maha-parinirvana*. Both drum and ayaka-platforms, the latter measuring 7.20 X2.10m, were covered with sculptured slabs. The dome, estimated to have a diameter of 42m, rested over the rim of the drum leaving all round a better of about 7.1m; its height being about half its diameter. Tall dome-slabs measuring about 2.32 m and carved with *tri-ratna* and *purna-kumbha,* covered the lower part of the dome, above which probably came the decorations in stucco".

The ornamental railing was about 4 m high and measured about 54 m in diameter, pierced on all the four sides by gateways. According to Dr. Barnet: "The railing consisted of about 244 m of coping resting on 136 pillars and 348 crossbars." Between the drum of the stupa and the railing was the paved circumambulatory path (*pradakshina-patha*) having a width of about 4 m.

Hiuen-Tsang who visited Dhanyakataka (Amaravati) in AD 639 says,[39] "The convents (*sangharamas*) are numerous, but are mostly deserted and ruined; of those preserved there are about 20 with 1000 or so priests. They all study the law of the Great Vehicle.":

The Amaravati *Maha-Chaitya* appears to have continued to be a living shrine for a long time. An eleventh century inscription records that a Pallava, Simhavarman worshipped the *Stupa*. Inscriptions in the nearby Amaresvara temple of the Kota chief, who ruled in 12th century-13th century from Dharanikota (Dhanyakataka), also refer to some donations to the *Maha-Chaitya*. One of these inscriptions dated to AD 1182 describes the *Maha-Chaitya* as a very lofty stupa, finely decorated with sculptures. Lastly, Dharmakirti, a pilgrim from Sri Lanka, visited Amaravati and carried out some repairs to the shrine in AD 1344. An inscription[40] to this effect has been found at Godaladeniya, near Kandy in Sri Lanka. Thus the mighty *stupa* survived almost intact, with its towering dome, till about the fourteenth century. After this, however, Amaravati Shrine was completely neglected and lost sight of.

The existence of the Amaravati *Stupa* came to light in 1797 when Collin Mackenzie visited Amaravati and found some men quarrying the remains of the stupa for materials for a new township being built by the Raja of Chintapalli, Raja Vasu Reddi Nayudu, who had shifted his residence a year earlier from Chintapalli to Amaravati. What Mackenzie saw was a 'great low mound crowned by a smaller one, some ninety feet in diameter and twenty feet high, and cased with bricks and slabs of stone". Mackenzie thought that the monument was a "mysterious structure" but he had no clear idea of its importance. Hence, he did not interfere. Consequently, many priceless sculptures were used in the Amaresvara temple, the Sivaganga tank and other buildings then being constructed while some were burnt for lime. Such vandalism continued for over 20 years till Mackenzie revisited the site in 1818, with a band of assistants and prepared drawings of the site and the stupa. He also recovered a few sculptured pieces.

After Mackenzie, many attempts were made to excavate the site. These were by Sir Walter Smith (1845), by Robert Sewell (1877), by James Burgess (1881) and thrice by Alexander Rea (1888-1889, 1905-1906 and 1908-1909). In spite of considerable spoilt for over hundred years, the potentiality of the Amaravati ruins was not exhausted. No wonder, the excavations undertaken during the year 1958-1959, by K.Subramanyam and K.Krishna Murthy of the Archaeological Survey of India, yielded a large number of inscribed architectural pieces, sculptured pieces, and other significant antiquities.

Nothing remains now of the grandest Amaravati *stupa* except a small mound which consists of just the drum of the brick-built stupa, the paved circumambulatory path and the circular alignment of the railing represented by a few uprights and pillars. At present, the stupa drum has a height of about 1.55 m and a diameter of 49.30m. However, a model of the *Maha Chaitya*, in its most evolved stage, the conjectural restoration of a part of the railing and a few sculptured panels, all in cement, may be seen in the courtyard of the nearby Museum.

The exhibits in the Amaravati Museum include those left at the site by Burgess (1881) and A.Rea (1888-89) and those recovered by K. Subramanyam and K. Krishna Murthy of the Archaeological Survey of India during the last excavations in 1958-59. Chronologically, the site Museum collection, mostly in stone, covers a period of 1500 years - from BC third century to AD twelfth century.

The main exhibit[41] in the Key-Gallery is "The lotus medallion, carved on a cross-bar of a railing datable to the second century AD. It is flanked on either side by a dome slab depicting the *purna-kumbha* or 'ambrosial with overflowing foliage and flowers'. Purna-Kumbha is an auspicious symbol expressing an idea of fulness and abundance".

The Western wing of the gallery is formed by two drum-slabs, each of them showing the bas-relief of a *stupa*. The stupa is shown encircled by a four-barred rail-cross-bars and fluted uprights showing lotus-medallions. On either side of the gateway is a seated lion atop an octagonal pillar. The ornate entrance to the *pradakshina-patha* is marked by a moon-stone carved with a lotus-design having *purna-kumbha* on either side. The *stupa* proper shows three out of the four *ayaka*-platforms, the front one surmounted by five pillars symbolizing five main events of Buddha's life. However, the principal object of worship is a *chakra* on a throne, flanked by *chauri* (flywhisk) - bearers and devotees.

There are atleast three Jatakas or the stories of the Buddha's former births sculptured on the dome of the Amaravati stupa. These are : the Mandhata-Jataka, the Sibi-Jataka and the Vessantara-Jataka. The Buddha recounted 547 tales of His former births. Each *Jataka* examplifies the Bodhisatta's efforts to develop virtue (*Paramita*) by doing good to others. For instance, once the Bodhisatta was born as King Sibi or Sivi and was reputed for his goodness and virtue. One day, a pigeon, chased by a hawk, rushed to the palace and sought protection of King Sibi. The hawk followed the pigeon to the royal court and demanded that pigeon should be given back to him as it was his lawful prey. The king declined to surrender the pigeon and instead struck a bargain to save the little bird's life. He gave the hawk a measure of his own flesh equal to the bird's weight. In the sculpture, the Sibi Jataka is portrayed in two panels-one showing the king giving shelter to the bird, and the other showing King Sibi about to cut out the required flesh from his thigh by a sword, to be weighed by a man standing to his left, with a balance in his hand.

The other drum-slab depicts a simple *stupa,* with three-barred rail and ayaka-pillars. Buddha is here symbolized variously as a flaming pillar (*agniskandha*), and wheel surmounting a pillar, each one placed on a throne. There are also two representations of *Buddha-pada* with umbrella on top.

A life-size standing image of Buddha greets the visitor as soon as he steps into gallery I. With left shoulder and forearm draped in *Sanghati,* his right hand, now missing, was probably in the *abhaya,* whereas his left hand holds the hem of the robe near his chest. A circular mark on the forehead, a mark of *Maha-purusha-lakshana* (sign of great man) is quite conspicuous. The top-knot and ring-like curls of the short hair, turned to the right are suggestive of superhuman wisdom. The image stands gracefully to a height of about 2 m (excluding the pedestal).

The drum slab near the southern wing depicts, in the foreground, the scene of the worship of wheel. On the dome of the stupa-relief are miniature compositions delineating scenes from the life of Gautama Buddha. These reliefs include the scenes of the descent of *Bodhisattva* in the form of a white elephant, Queen Mayadevi's dream of the elephant entering her womb, the interpretation of the dream, the birth of Siddhartha and the presentation of the baby before *nagara-devatas*. In a running frieze below, occurs the story of the *Mandhata-jataka* in four panels.

Another impressive piece in this gallery is an ornate cross-bar. Both its faces are carved: on the obverse is carved the lotus-medallion while the reverse shows the scene of the presentation of Rahula to Buddha. In the scene carved within an outline of lotus-petals, Buddha has been represented symbolically by a throne, his *padukas* below the throne and a flaming pillar surmounted by the *triratna*. A crowd of monks, is seen to the left of the throne, while on the right is a group of women from royal household. A princely figure is seen presenting Rahula to Buddha. Behind him, in half-turned attitude, stands gracefully Yasodhara pointing her hand at her son urging him to ask for his inheritance.

Occupying the pride of place in gallery-II is a limestone stele with labelled bas-reliefs of the second century B.C.

The reliefs on the southern face contain six scenes pertaining to the last three months of the life of Buddha - from his stay at Vaisali to the *Parinirvana* at Kusinagara. On the left corner occurs the representation of the *Bahuputa-chaitya*, a favourite resort of Gautama Buddha. In these scenes chaitya has been represented as a tree - within-railing. The most prominent of the three trees is worshipped by two devotees, one of them with folded hands and the other holding a child in the out-stretched left hand. It has an inscribed label giving the name *Bahuputa-chaitya*. To the right of the first scene is a kneeling figure with folded hands before a *Buddha-pada*. The label calls it *Chapala-chaitya*, another favourite resort of Buddha at Vaisali. Over the second scene is a vaulted structure with three pinnacles, and outside a *Buddha-pada* under an umbrella. The inscription on the vault says 'The Lord dwells in the Kutagara cottage in Mahavana at Vaisali'. It is said that Buddha went from *Chapala-Chaitya* to *Mahavana-Kutagara* and from there, while bidding farewell to Vaisali, gazed at the city 'with an elephant's look', the actual inscription also states nagapalogana. The next scene is represented by a river with a handled bowl; beside it is an ablong seat below a tree. As the story goes, Buddha fell sick on his way to Kusinagara. He sat under a tree and wanted to drink water from the adjoining streamlet. As the water was muddy, Ananda, his disciple, was hesitant but on Buddha's insistence he went to fetch water. To his surprise Ananda saw that the streamlet had begun to flow clear. The river shown in the relief stands for this streamlet where miracle of clear water took place. A fragment of the last scene, the *Parinirvana* at Kusinagara, is only preserved but the label says 'the extinction of the Lord in the *sala*-grove'.

The second face gives a few scenes from Sravasti including the familiar scene of the purchase of Jetavana park by Anathapindika from prince Jeta; all with appropriate lebels. Another scene delineated here relates to Dhanyakataka on the bank of the river Krishna. It is interesting to note that the Krishna has been depicted here as if taking a turn, which is true even today. A part of the ancient city with buildings and chaitya-windows is also shown.

A drum-frieze containing a donative inscription depicts the scenes from Buddha's life. The first scene shows water indicated by wavy lines symbolizing Anotatta lake associated with Maya's conception. Other three represent *Bodhi-tree* symbolizing Buddha's Enlightenment, worship of Dharma-Chakra (First Sermon), and *Stupa*- with worshippers (Parinirvana).

There is also an inscription on the octagonal pillar which speaks of the installation of a *Dharma-Chakra* at the eastern side of the *Maha-Chaitya* at Dhanyakataka for the Purvasailiya monks. A Telugu inscription of the Twelfth century is engraved on the other side of the Brahmi inscription.

Majority of the surviving Amaravati sculptures are in the Government Museum, Madras. This collection is largely the one excavated by James Burgess in 1881 and some sculptures discovered by Alexander Rea who excavated the site thrice in 1888-1889, 1905-1906, and 1908-1909. There are as many as 72 sculptures depicting scenes from Buddha's Life, and 27 sculptures depicting Buddha's Previous Lives (Jatakas and Avadanas) in the Madras Museum. These sculptures[42] in marble and limestone cover a period of over 450 years from about BC 200 to AD 250.

Who were the people who created these marvellous Buddhist shrines and sculptures of Amaravati? The answer to this vexed question has been given by the donors themselves who have left a record of their names and status in life by way of inscriptions (in Prakrit) covering a period of about 450 years. As many as one hundred and twenty-five inscriptions[43] found on the Amaravati sculptures preserved in the Government Museum, Madras, speak volumes of the devotion of the early Buddhists. Most of the inscriptions at Amaravati open with the auspicious words "*Sidham*" (Success), and some of them after this begin with "Adoration to the Lord; the illuminator (`lit. Sun) of the World" (*namo bhagavato logaticasa*) or "Adoration to the Lord Buddha, the best of all beings" (*namo bhagavato savasatutamasa Budhasa*). The gifts are invariably termed as "*suciya dana*" (Pious gift) or "*deyadhamma*" (Meritorious gift). Many donors[44] dedicate their gifts (*danam*) to their kith and kin while some dedications are "for the welfare and happiness of the whole world" (*ca lokasa hitasukhathataya*). An inscription says; "At the foot of the great caitya of the Lord has been placed a lamp pillar, as seat of merit" (*bhagavato mahaceitya padamale apano dhamathana divakhabho patithavito*).

The inscriptions mention monks (*bhadata*), elders (*thera*), mendicants (*pendapatika*), worthy men (*aya*), lay worshippeers male and female (*uvasaka* and *uvasika*) disciples male and female (*atevasika* and *atevasikini*), preachers of the law (*dhamakathika*), supervisors of renovation works (*navakamaka*), householders (*gahapati*), housewives (*grahani*), generals (*senagopa*), perfumers (*gadhika*), leather-workers (*camakara*), whole towns (*negama*), and many others. The names of the donors also reflect in an ample measure the influence of Buddhism on the lives of the people. The names particularly derived from the Buddha, the Dhamma and the Sangha are; Bodhi, Bodhika, Budha (3), Budharajida (2), Buddharakhita (4), Buddhi (2), Dhama, Dhamadina, Dhamarakhita, Dhamasarayana, Dhamasiria, Dhamila, Sanghada, Sanghamita, Sangharakhishita, Sangharakhita, Sanghada. Other Buddhistic names are: Ananda, Bala, Mahadhamakhadika, Makabuddhia, Nagabudhia, Nagasena, Rahula, and Siddhatha (Siddhartha).

Nagarjunakonda

Nagarjunakonda, like Amaravati, is also situated on the bank of river Krishna in district Guntur of Andhra Pradesh.

Traditionally, Nagarjunakonda is associated with Acharya Nagarjuna, the renowned founder of the Madhyamika (Sunyavada) School of Buddhist philosophy. According to an ancient Tibetan tradition, Nagarjuna, towards the evening of his life, lived at Nagarjunakonda and was interred there. Hiuen Tsang gives an interesting description of the monastery said to have been built by the Satavahana King Gautamiputra Yajnasri Satakarni (AD 166-196) for Nagarjuna at Sriparvata, now known as Nagarjunakonda.

The valley of Nagarjunakonda became a flourishing Buddhist centre in AD third century largely due to the patronage of the Ikshvaku Kings and Queens. The Ikshvakus claimed their descent from the mythological Ikshvakus of Ayodhya. Chamtasri, sister of the founder of this royal house, Vasishthiputra Siri Chamtamula, was an ardent devotee of the Buddha. This pious lady and other Ikshvaku Princesses were, therefore, the main donors of the Buddhist shrines in and around Vijayapuri, the Ikshvaku capital.

The second Ikshvaku King, Virapurushadatta, is said to have embraced Buddhism. His son and successor, Ehuvala Chamtamula II, was also a Buddhist. Like his father, he ruled for 24 years. His reign marked the golden period of Nagarjunakonda as it was during this period that construction of Buddhist shrines reached its peak. The construction of Buddhist shrines at Nagarjunakonda came to an end in the eleventh regnal year of Rudrapurusha-datta, the last known Ikshvaku King.

More than thirty Buddhist shrines came up in the Nagarjunakonda valley during the Ikshvaku rule. It was the largest and the most important settlement in South India in AD third century.

The Maha- Chaitya (*Stupa*) was the first and the foremost magnificent shrine to be constructed at Nagarjunakonda. The Maha-Chaitya (Site 1), and its allied units took about a decade to reach its final form, and all the time it received the munificence of the pious lady Chamtasri, the sister of Vasisthiputra Chamtamula, although the actual construction was done under the supervision of one, the Reverend Ananda. Built in the sixth regnal year of Virapurushadatta, the *Stupa* wheel-shaped on plan, had a diameter of about 27.5 m. with ayaka platforms surmounted by ayaka-pillars at the four cardinal directions.

Basically, it was a *saririka* (corporeal) *Stupa*, for it disclosed a reliquary including a tooth-relic, and the inscription alludes to it as the *dhatu* or bodily remains of Lord Buddha (*samma-sambudhasa dhatuvara-parigahita*). The *Maha-Vihara* and the apsidal *Chaitya Griha* (Stupa-shrine) meant for a much smaller Stupa were set-up respectively in the fifteenth and the eighteenth regnal years of the same king for the Aparamahavinaseliya sect. Some establishments nearby were built between the sixth and the fifteenth regnal years, for one Bodhisri, a layworshipper from Govagama, donated an apsidal Stupa shrine in the fourteenth regnal year of Virapurushadatta to the Ceylonese monastery (Site 43) on the Chula-Dhammagiri. Besides this, Upasika Bodhisri also built a chaitya-hall at the Kulaha-*Vihara*, a shrine for the Bodhi-tree at the Sihala-*Vihara*, one cell at the Great Dhammagiri, a mandava-pillar at the *Mahavihara*, a hall for religious practice at the Devagiri, a tank, verandah and great *chaitya* at Kantakasela, three cells at Hiramuthuva, seven cells at Papila, a stone mandava at Puphagiri - *Vihara*.

The glorious rise of Nagarjunakonda in AD third century looks like a golden page from history. With the downfall of the Ikshvakus in the early years of AD fourth century, Nagarjunakonda relapsed into darkness, its shrines, its artistic tradition, and its contacts with the Buddhist world—all vanished.[45]

The Nagarjunakonda monuments, the treasure trove of Buddhist art and culture, remained unknown for centuries and came to light only in March, 1926 when A.R.Saraswati, Telugu Assistant to the Archaeological Superintendent for Epigraphy, Archaeological Survey of India, discovered this site. A.H. Longhurst, Superintendent, Archaeological Survey of India, Southern Circle was the first to commence excavation here in 1927 which continued till February 1932. He discovered a number of Buddhist monasteries. In 1938 a limited operation was carried out by T.N. Ramachandran.

Nagarjunakonda assumed importance in the 1950's when the construction of the Nandikonda project was conceived as a result of which the valley was to be transformed into a reservoir. In order to salvage, whatever possible, of the priceless art treasure, which the Ikshvakus had created more than 1600 years ago, a special project for extensive excavation was formed in August 1954. Accordingly, R. Subramanyam, a Superintendent of the Archaeological Survey of India, excavated the entire valley within a short span of six years exposing about 120 sites.

All the sites now stand submerged by the gigantic multipurpose Nagarjunasagar Dam. Yet the glory of Nagarjunakonda shines in the midst of the third largest man-made lake in the world. Hundreds of beautiful sculptures and some of the monuments which would have been submerged by the construction of the dam have been lifted to the top of a hill, which stands right in the midst of the reservoir. The island museum, which is unique and first of its kind in the world, can be reached by a launch from Anuppu, the jetty point about 8 km from Vijayapuri, a little town which has sprung up around the dam. From Anupu, Nagarjunakonda is about 14 km. The Nagarjunasagar dam is 150 km by road from Hyderabad, the capital of Andhra Pradesh.

The most attractive piece[46] in the Key-Gallery of the Museum is the colossal statue of Lord Buddha standing to a height of about 3 m. Originally found in several fragments at Site 4, the image, like any other sculpture from Nagarjunakonda, stands in frontal pose holding the hem of his garment in the left hand, while the right hand (broken) is granting protection.

On the eastern wing of the key-gallery is the panel depicting the main episodes of Buddha's life. In its elegant style of execution as well as in the portrayal of human moods the relief ranks as one of the best specimens of Nagarjunakonda art.

A bust of Buddha notable for its sharp features, is the first exhibit to be seen on the other side of the gallery, which has a number of architectural pieces like the cornice-beam, coping-stone and *ayaka-pata*. The gods carrying away in procession the relinquished crown of the Buddha at the time of his great renunciation is the theme depicted within a medallion on an *ayaka-pata*. In the next exhibit are carved the scenes of conversion of Nanda, cousin of Buddha. It is one of the finest pieces of Nagarjunakonda showing from right to left the scenes of the meeting of Nanda and his wife Sunderi with Buddha, tonsure ceremony for Nanda's ordination, Buddha flying to heaven with Nanda and the final conversion.

The next exhibit is a drum-slab carved with a developed form of a *stupa*. It is followed by a cornice-beam depicting, the five important life-events of Gautama Buddha, viz., Birth, Great Renunciation, Mara's attack, First Sermon at Sarnath and *Mahaparinirvana*. On the next slab is to be seen the serpent king Muchalinda, a favourite motif of the Nagarjunakonda artists.

The sculptures in the northern wing of the Main Gallery depict the Jataka tales carved variously on drum-slabs, dome-slabs and cornice beams. The sculptures preserved here relate to eight Jatakas, namely, Sasa Jataka, Champeyya Jataka, Sibi Jataka,

Mandhata Jataka, Mahapadma Jataka, Vessantara Jataka, Dasartha Jataka, and Mahahamasa Jataka.

The *Sasa-Jataka* depicts the story when Bodhisatta was born in one of his earliest births as a hare. His friends are a monkey, a jackal and an otter. On a full-moon day, the otter brings fish, the jackal a lizard and milk, and the monkey some mangoes as gifts for the guests. The hare, the Bodhisatta, however, decides to offer himself as gift. And when the god Sakra, disguised as brahmin, asks for something to eat, the hare leaps into the fire in order to roast himself, but the fire does not burn him. Sakra then explains how he has come to put him (the hare) to test. This Jataka is depicted on a mutilated drum-slab.

The *Champeyya Jataka* is the story when Bodhisatta was born as a serpent-king who allowed himself to be caught by a snake-charmer as he did not want to break his vows of virtue. He was finally rescued by his queen Sumana by requesting King Uggarsena of Banaras (Varanasi) to intercede on his behalf. Here, the story is represented in four panels on the cornice beam, beginning with the catching of the snake from an ant-hill by the snake-charmer.

The *Sibi-Jataka* has already been described under Amaravati. At Nagarjunakonda, the sculpture shows that as the flesh cut by the king Sibi was not sufficient, the king himself sits on the pan of the balance. Thereupon, the gods Sakra and Agni appear in their real forms and laud the king.

The *Mandhata-Jataka* is the story of the ambitious king who was in possession of the seven gems - a wheel, an elephant, a horse, a gem, a wife, a householder and a minister. On reaching heaven, he even shared the throne with the god Sakra. Not satisfied with that, the king wanted to oust Sakra. This evil thought causes him to fall down from heaven in a park of his capital-city.

The *Mahapadama-Jataka* is the story when the Bodhisatta was born as a son of king Brahmandatta of Varanasi. The queen, who is the step-mother of Padmakumara, the handsome son of the king of Varanasi, is enamoured of him, but the prince does not respond to his overtures. The frustrated queen makes a false complaint to the king of molesting her by the prince to the king. Under the orders of the king, the prince is thrown down the robber's cliff but the naga king protects the virtuous prince. The prince then turns into an ascetic. On knowing the actual facts later, the king requested the prince Padmakumara to return to Varanasi and take over the kingdom but the prince declines the offer. This story is depicted in three panels on the dome-slab.

The *Vessantara* Jataka tells how Prince Vessantara, then Bodhisatta, had great craving to give in charity whatever he possessed. One day, taking advantage of his generosity, eight brahmins from Kalinga, where there was a severe drought, came to Vessantara to beg his white elephant. When he parted with the State elephant, who had the magical power to bring peace, prosperity and rain, the people protested and the king had to banish him. His wife Madra, and their two children also accompanied him in the chariot. On the way he made a gift of his chariot and horses to the brahmins who begged for the same. Thus the family had to go on foot. Then another brahmin appeared and asked for the children, the prince gave them as well. The *Vessantara jataka* is depicted on a drum slab bearing the representation of an ornamental stupa.

The *Dasartha-Jataka* is the story of King Dasartha and his two sons Rama, Lakshmana and a daughter Sita.

The *Mahahamsa-Jataka,* depicted on a mandapa pillar, tells the story of queen Khema and king Samyama of Varanasi when they took fancy for two golden geese flying in the air. As per their orders, a hunter caught them and brought them to the palace. One of the two birds, Sumukha, the goose-king, preached *Dhamma* to the king and queen.

Several dome slabs in the southern and western wings depict the important life scenes of the Buddha. In the upper compartment of a dome-slab is shown the scene in which

Sumedha, who resides in the *Tushita* heaven as Bodhisattva, resolving to take his final birth on earth. The lower compartment depicts his descent in a heavenly chariot as a white elephant, accompanied by celestial musicians, to enter the body of Maya. There are several scenes, carved on a cornice-beam, which present vividly the subsequent events. Birth in Lumbini garden; Asita examines the child, who is represented by a pair of feet on the cloth, and predicts that he would be a Buddha when grown up. Siddhartha witnesses four visions that led to his renunciation-in the scene Indra spreads parasol on him, four guardians of the directions hold hoofs of the horse on palms so that there is no noise; musicians and bearers carrying flag-staff and fly-whisk accompany him. Then on the banks of the river Anoma, he changes his garments for a monk's dress. And Gods carry away the relinquished crown of the Buddha.

Siddhartha practises penances for six years, at the end of which, at Uruvela (Bodh-Gaya), he accepts milk and rice from Sujata, and sits under the Bodhi-tree determined not to give up seat until he has gained full insight. Mara, the Evil One, attacks him but has to retreat. Eventually, he attains enlightenment and becomes Buddha. Then the Buddha proceeds to Sarnath where he propounds his doctrine. In course of time, Buddha visits Kapilavastu and approaches the apartments of Yasodhara who stands waiting at the door. Rahula enquires of him about inheritance. Buddha goes to the heaven to preach to his mother Maya. Also, he converts the robber Angulimala, the king Ajatasatru, the *naga* of Uruvela, and the *Yaksha* Alavaka.

A few monuments have been faithfully reconstituted out of ancient materials on the Nagarjunakonda Island. These are:Maha-stupa and apsidal shrine, Site I: monastery, Site 4: apsidal shrine, Site 43: and stupa with swastika inset, Site 59.

Other Shrines

Bhattiprolu, near Rapalle in Krishna district, was one of the earliest Buddhist shrines in Andhra. The remains of the stupa discovered here revealed that it had a diameter of 132 feet with an additional basement of 8 feet wide running all around. During the excavations in 1891, a rock-crystal inscribed casket containing sacred relics of the Buddha was discovered here. These relics were presented by the Government of India to the Maha Bodhi Society of India, and the same were enshrined in the *Dharmarajika Vihara* constructed by the Maha Bodhi Society at Calcutta in 1920.

Jaggayyapeta, in the Nandigama Taluk of the Krishna district, was another important Buddhist centre in ancient Andhra. Some inscriptions of the 2nd century BC as well as some inscriptions of the Ikshvaku period, the third century AD, discovered here amply prove that Jaggayyapeta was a flourishing Buddhist centre for a long time. An inscription by a lay Buddhist devotee of the reign of Sri Virapurisadata says[47]:

"Success! On the 10th day of the 8th fortnight of the rainy season, in the 20th year of the king Purisadata (Purushadatta), the glorious hero (Śrivira) of the Ikshvakus and son of the Madhara (mother) - the artisan (avesam) Sidatha (Siddhartha) resident in the village of Mahakamudurura, the son of the artisan Naka Chamda (Nagachandra) resident in the village of Nadatura in the province (ratha) of Kammaka, having associated (with him) his mother....and his wife....and his son....and his daughter....and his brother....and his wife....and their two sons....and daughter, erected this, together with the multitude of his blood-relations, friends and connections, in the village of Velagiri, near the eastern gate of the great chaitya of divine Buddha, five (5) Ayaka-pillars, which were dedicated by all (the above persons), as his own meritorious gift for the good and the welfare of all living beings."

A number of interesting Buddhist sculptures from Jaggayyapeta, Bhattiprolu, Goli and Ghantasala are now preserved in the Government Museum, Madras (Tamil Nadu).

A few antiquities discovered from Alluru, Gummadidurru and Lingarajapalli can be seen in the Archaeological Museum at Amaravati. The sculptured slabs from Gummadiduru include a chaitya-slab on which are depicted the worship of dharma-chakra and scenes from the *Mandhata-Jataka* and scenes from the *Chhaddanta-Jataka.*

The sole surviving Buddhist symbol from Lingarajapalli is a big sandstone wheel with a diameter of 1.10 metres. It has a circular hub with twenty-eight spokes emanating from it. The outer periphery bears decoration of *triratnas*.

At Guntapalli, 45 km from Ellore railway station in the West Godavari district, there are two Buddhist caves. These were probably excavated around 200 BC or even earlier, and are thus one of the earliest caves in India. Besides these rock-cut shrines, Gunatapalli also has the ruins of two brick-built *viharas*, a *chaitya-hall* and several *stupas* of various sizes.

At Sankaram hill, 3 km north of Ankapalli railway station in Visakhapatnam district, there are four Buddhist caves. Three of them have carvings of the Buddha and the fourth has a *stupa*. The facade of the fourth cave has a seated Buddha under a *chaitya arch*. These caves are believed to have been excavated in about AD 350. Sankaram has also a number of monolithic *stupas;* and the remains of an extensive structural monastery. One of them being 65 feet in diameter at the base. There are also remains of an extensive structural monastery at Sankaram.

The latest Buddhist sites to be excavated (1986) in Andhra Pradesh are at Bavikonda and Nelakondapalli. Bavikonda is on the seashore of Bheemmunipatnam in Visakhapatnam district. The excavations at Bavikonda[48] have brought to light one *mahastupa*, seven minor *stupas* and a *vihara* consisting of 51 rooms, a huge congregation hall, a library and some rock-cut troughts and a small grinding stone evidently used for preparing some herbal medicines. This shows that Bavikonda complex was not only an important religious centre but also an important education and medical centre. At Nelakondapalli in Khammam district has been found one of the biggest Buddhist stupas in South India. The *stupa* was built of wholly large-size burnt bricks.

(IV) THE BUDDHIST LEGACY

Following the decline of Buddhism in Andhra, many Buddhist shrines were converted by the Brahmins into Hindu temples. Two of the major Buddhist Chaityas converted into Hindu temples have been identified by the scholars with the Kopetesvara temple at Chezarla in Guntur district and the Trivikrama temple at Ter in Western Deccan. Both these structures are still standing in entirety as built by the Buddhists. K.R. Srinivasan says[49]: "Fortunately there are two apsidal shrines of original Buddhist dedication and subsequent conversion to the Hindu creed, still existing in their entirety. They are the Trivikrama temple at Ter, in Western Deccan, and the Kopetesvara temple at Chejerla, in coastal Andhra. Both are dated earlier than 600 A.D., but not earlier than 300 A.D. Of the two, the Kopetesvara may be the earlier one judged from the stylistic and architectural point of view. This *Chaitya* built of large-sized bricks shows no external pilaster on its wall, except at the two front ends which are not original. Internally the ceiling of stone slabs is supported by a system of ten stone pillars, ranged five each along the straight sides of the apsidal structure and spanned by thick stone beams".

Draksharama, near Ramachandrapuram in East Godavari district is another Buddhist Chaitya converted into a Hindu temple. Supporting the belief that this temple was originally a Buddhist shrine, N. Ramesan says[50]: "The third legend about this temple is that the temple was originally a Buddha *Chaitya* and that during the course of revival of Hindu worship, it was converted into a Hindu temple. The *Mula Virat* or the *Linga* is said to be one of the *Ayaka Stambhas* of the original Buddha *Chaitya*. Chaityas or stupas in Buddhist methods of worship, are mounds raised over the corporeal relics of Lord Buddha or a great Acharya. Buddhist Stupas and Chaityas are spread all over India, but one of the main characteristics of the Andhra type of Chaityas and Stupas is the existence of the five vertical pillars, called the *Ayaka Stambhas,* which are erected in the four cardinal directions viz., East, South, West and North. In all the Chaityas of Andhra, this is a peculiar characteristic which is found. These *Ayaka Stambhas* which are five in number, are said to represent the five major incidents in the life of Lord Buddha viz., *Janama* or Birth, *Mahabhinis-kramana* or the great renunciation, *Samyak-Sambodhi* or the prefect realisation, *Dharma Chakra Pravarthana* or the setting in motion of the wheel of *Dharma*, and *Mahaparinirvana* or the final absorption of Lord Buddha into the Infinite. The *Ayaka Stambhas* are generally vertical pillars made of white marble stone. Andhra Desa and especially the Krishna river basin has been a famous seat of Buddhism, and many stupas have been found in this valley as for example at Amravathi, Goli, Jaggayyapeta, Ghantasala etc., not to speak of the Mahachaitya at Nagarjuna-konda. During the period of the revival of Hindu worship, some of these Chaityas were converted and re-adopted to Hindu worship. For example, in the *Garbha Griha* of the Amaraswara temple of Amaravathi in Guntur district, there is typical white marble lotus medallion slab of the Buddhist type. The peculiar characteristic Buddhist type of bricks are also found in the temple. It is therefore possible that the Buddhist *Chaitya* and the *Ayaka Stambhas* have been re-converted into a Hindu temple and adapted for *linga* worship."

How at Amaravati, Draksharama and other places, the Buddhist pillars (*Ayhaka Stambhas*) were shaped by the Hindus to serve the purpose of a *Linga* has been well described by Dr. I.K. Sarma. He says[51]: "Amaravati - Dharanikota grew with a Buddhist base right from a Pre-Mauryan period. This very place came to be regarded as an *arama-kshetra* with the Amaresvara *Linga* as the presiding deity of the *Sthala*. The toponym Amaravati itself is regarded as a corrupt form of "Aramavati". It is not without significance that the long east coast covered by Godavari-Krishna deltas, located mid-way between the Magadha (the home of Buddhism) and Ceylon (the strong-hold of Buddhism) developed *aramakshetras*. We have known at least five such *aramas*. These are Draksharama and Kurmarama, both in East Godavari district; Somarama and Ksirarama, in West Godavari district and Amararama in Guntur district. In each of these places a vast temple complex for Siva was raised by Bhima-I (812-821 A.D.) the Eastern Chalukyan monarch. An unusually tall *Linga* was consecrated in the Sanctum which is a double storeyed Sarvatobhadrika shrine. Several *Angalyas* tall *prakara* walls with *dalans* were added by the successive rulers. An examination of such a *Linga* within the Amaresavra temple, Amaravati itself has revealed that the upper most part of the *Linga,* which is nearly six metre high, has a square mortise hole although rounded off and in the remaining four places too (also Adikesvara temple, Chebrolu, Guntur district), the *Linga* within the main sanctum was similarly tall and of Palnad lime stone. There is no doubt that a Buddhist pillar (*ayaka* or *mandapa Khambha*) was shaped to a *linga* in all these cases."

Srisailam, situated in the thick forests of the Nallamalai Hills in Andhra is yet another Buddhist shrine converted into a Hindu temple. The tribal population around Srisailam is largely of the Chenchu tribe. The Chenchus were once ardent Buddhists and had their shrine at Srisailam which is now a Shiva temple. Significantly enough, the Chenchus still have the right to worship in this temple independent of all the Brahmin priests. To quote N. Ramesan again[52]: "The Chenchus (the tribal people who live in this part of the hills) have free permission, even today, to go into any part of the temple, including the *Garbha Griha,* enshrining the sacred *linga*. It is in fact, this tribal people, that help to drag the car in the big *ratha* festival of the temple and also at other minor services within the temple. During the great Sivarathri festival, when thousands of people congregate here, to bathe in the sacred waters of the Patalganga and worship Lord Mallikarjuna, the Chenchus also go and worship inside the *Garbha Griha* independent of all the priests. To this day, caste, creed or sex, does not prohibit any one, providing he or she is a Hindu, from doing *Abhiseka* to the Lord from the waters of Patalganga or to do *Archana* with flowers directly. Such a catholic form of worship is unknown anywhere else in Andhra, except at Srisailam, and this custom probably dates back to the Buddhist period when caste rules were not so rigid".

N. Ramesan adds[53]: "Srisailam may be traced back to the Buddhist period and perhaps even earlier than to the Mahayana school of Buddhism which is known to have flourished during the first century A.D. The Buddhist pilgrims, Fa Hian and Hieun Tsang have made reference to the Sriparvatha hill which is in the Nagarjunakonda valley of the same river Krishna. After the decline of Buddhism, the Hindu religion would appear to have re-established its authority, probably due to the efforts of Adi Sankara, and Srisailam which is a seat of Hindusim, is now counted as one of the sacred *Kshetras* with an important seat for `*Sakti* in the name of *Mahadevi* which later on came to be called as *Brahmarambha*".

The famous shrine of Balaji or Lord Venkatesvara at Tirupati at a height of about 2800 feet among the seven hills on the Eastern Ghats in Andhra is also believed to be a Buddhist shrine. All sources combined, the points in favour of this identification can be briefly summed up as follows.

Hiuen Tsang mentions three important Buddhist centres in Andhra Pradesh, viz. Dhanyakataka, Sriparvata and Potalka. Of these, the first two stand fully identified with Amaravati and Nagarjunakonda, and the third, Potalka[54] is identified by some scholars with the Tirupati hills, which were also known earlier as Pullikunran or the hill of the Chieftain Pulli. The Pullis have been identified[55] with the Kalavars or Kalabhras, who were Buddhists, and migrated from Tirupati to Kanchipuram in Tamil Nadu where they ruled for nearly three centuries.

Hiuen Tsang has described Potalka in these words[56]:

"To the east of the Malaya mountains in Mount *Po-to lo-kia* (Potalka). The passes of this mountain are very dangerous; its sides are precipitous, and its valleys rugged. On the top of the mountain is a lake; its waters are clear as a mirror. From a hollow proceeds a great river which encircles the mountain as flows down twenty times and then enters the southern sea. By the side of the lake is a rock-palace of the Devas. Here Avalokitesvara in coming and going, takes his abode. Those who strongly desire to see this Bodhisattva do not regard their lives, but crossing the water (*fording the streams*), climb the mountain forgetful of its difficulties and dangers; of those who make the attempt there are very few who reach the summit. But even of those who dwell below the mountain, if they earnestly pray and beg to behold the god, sometimes he appears as Tsz'tsai-t'ien (*Isvara-deva*), sometimes under the form of a Yogi (a *Pamsupata*); he address them with benevolent words and then they obtain their wishes according to their desires".

Tirupati is not mentioned as a Hindu shrine in any earlier Brahmanical text; neither the Puranas nor the Mahabharata refer to it. The Sangam poets also do not refer to any shrine at Tirupati, though festivals are mentioned. Since there is no history of Balaji, the Brahmins claim that the image or murthi of Balaji is self-manifested. The device of 'self-manifestation of murthi' is the usual device adopted by the Brahmins while converting the Buddhist shrines as Hindu shrines.

The image of Lord Balaji does not resemble any of the Vishnu images as it is in fact an image of the Bodhisattva Avalkotesvara as described by Hiuen Tsang. Another view is that the deity of Balaji is the image of the Buddha. A.R. Kulkarni says[57]: "The worship of the deity of Balaji in the famous Tirupathi Temple in Andhra Pradesh is also the worship of Buddha. The Dasera or the 10th day of Ashwin (Bright fort-night) is celebrated as the birthday of Balaji. It may be here remember that Dasera is the birthday of Buddha according to Hindu tradition. From the fact that the birthday of both Balaji and the Buddha is the 10th day of Ashwin, we can legitimately infer that Balaji is Buddha".

It seems that at the time of Hiuen Tsang in the seventh century, the Buddhist shrine atop Tirupati was in the process of being Hinduised. Since it was lying unattended, both the Shaivas and Vaishnavas tried to claim the shrine. This dispute continued for centuries and there was even a Court case in the eleventh century. Ultimately, the Vaishnavaṣ became victorious when Ramanuja, the Vaishnava saint, who stayed at Tirupati for sometime in the 12th century, managed to place the weapons, *sankha* and *chakra,* in the hands of the image of Balaji, and introduced the Vaishnava worship.

By the time this happened, the Buddha had been inducted into the Hindu pantheon, as ninth *Avatara* of Vishnu. Hence, there was no difficulty for Ramanuja to declare it a Vaishnava shrine.

While adopting the Buddhist shrines to their use, the Hindus had to compromise in certain cases and retain some of the Buddhistic practices and traditions. The most important Buddhist practice retained at Tirupati is the practice of tonsure. Here not only men but also women undergo tonsure. This practice is unique only to Tirupati. There is no doubt that it is a Buddhist legacy. As a rule, shaven-headed men and women are inauspicious in Hinduism but tonsure is an essential condition for Buddhist monks and nuns. Even lay Buddhists resort to tonsure on certain occasions. Hence, it has to be conceded that the Brahmins had to retain this practice in view of the popularity of the tonsure amongst the Buddhists.

All this evidence leads to only one conclusion, that is, the present day temple of Lord Balaji at Tirupati was once a Buddhist shrine.

Apart from appropriating a large number of Buddhist shrines in Andhra, the Hindus adopted and absorbed a number of Buddhistic customs and practices also. As we have seen earlier, almost all the inscriptions by the donors found at Amaravati and Nagarjunakonda begin with the auspicious words "*Siddham*" or 'Success'. Because of this usage by the devout Buddhists, the Buddhist culture during the Satavahana period and after came to be known as "*Siddham Namah*" culture. And when Buddhism was ousted from Andhra, the Hindus found it difficult to do away with the '*Siddham Namah*' formula. So they prefaced it with the name of Siva and transformed it into "*Om namah Sivaya Siddham Namah*[58]". And this is so even today.

(V) THE REVIVAL MOVEMENT

The Buddhist revival movement began in Andhra only after 1956 in the wake of the mass movement initiated by Dr. B.R. Ambedkar. The pioneer Bhikkhu to propagate Buddhism in

Andhra Pradesh was Venerable Şumedha Vimalaksha. Born in Bengal, he came to Guntur as a Sramnera in early 1960's and established an organisation by name "Baudha *Vihara* Saraswati Samithi" at Guntur, and began propagating Teachings of the Buddha in Andhra Pradesh, the renowned land of Buddhist shrines of Amaravati and Nagarjunakonda. Ven. Sumedha also established another *Vihara* known as "Nagarjuna Buddha *Vihara*" at Hindupur, Rayalseema. He also published scores of books and pamphlets in English and Telugu.

The other important Buddha *Viharas* in Andhra are: Jetavana Buddha *Vihara*, Secunderabad; Anand Buddha *Vihara*, Sai Nagar, North Lala Guda, Secundrabad. Ven. Bhikkhu Sangharakhita is the resident monk in this *Vihara*; Maha Pragya *Vihara*, Boktapur, Adilabad District, Ven. Bhikkhu Sanghanand is the resident monk in this *Vihara*; and Siddhartha *Vihara*, Kancherapalem, Visakhapatnam.

Another pioneer organisation to preach and progagate Dhamma in modern Andhra is the Buddhist Cultural Organisation, Alankar Side Lane, Nagarampalem, Guntur. It was founded by B. Veerabhadra Rao in December 1955. As there is acute dearth of Buddhist literature in the local language, Telugu, this organisation has done a laudable work of bringing out more than thirty pamphlets for wider circulation, most of which have been compiled or translated by Veerabhadra himself. The Buddhist Cultural Organisation is quite active at the National level as well as at International level. The two all Andhra Pradesh Buddhist Conferences organised by it in 1980 and 1986 at Hyderabad and Guntur respectively have brought cohesion in the Buddhist revival movement in the State.

There are atleast three more Buddhist Societies engaged in the noble task of preaching and preserving the Buddha-Dhamma in Andhra Pradesh. These are: Andhra Buddhist Society, Kancherapalem, Vishakhapatnam; Andhra Buddhist Association, Antar Gaon Textiles, Karimnagar District; and Buddha Sangha, Kodak Pura, Boyanapally, Secundrabad.

The Buddhist revival movement is slowly but steadily marching ahead in Andhra. In 1951, there were only 230 Buddhists in Andhra Pradesh. This figure rose to 6,753 in 1961. And in 1981, Andhra had as many as 12,930 Buddhists.

A major landmark in modern Andhra is the erection of a giant statue of Lord Buddha by the Government of Andhra Pradesh. This 60 feet high standing statue of the Buddha will be installed on the Gibraltor Rock in the middle of the picturesque Hussainsagar lake situated in the heart of the twin cities of Hyderabad and Secunderabad.

Notes and References

1. Cf. N.S. Ramaswami, Indian Monuments, New Delhi, p. 123.

   The text of the multilated inscription is as follows:

   "In the future world..... annointed.
   Indeed (it) has been written here by me that people....many.
   They regret. Therefore... by me.
   When one gets victory (in a battle or war).
   And then again of myself also.
   Too ..... there."
2. Romila Thapar, Asoka and the Decline of the Mauryas, second edition, Delhi, 1973, p. 256.
3. K.A. Nilakanta Sastri, A History of South India, Fourth Edition, Madras, 1984, p. 88.
4. Epigraphica Indica, VIII, p. 93. The inscription reads as :

   "Sadavahanakule kane rajini Nasika kena

   Samanana mahamatena lena karita..."
5. Epigraphica Indica, VIII, p. 73.
6. Ibid.
7. Epigraphica Indica, X, Appendix - A List of Brahmi inscriptions by H. Ludders, Calcutta, 1969 edition, Nos. 1086-1108.
8. Ibid., Ludders List Nos. 1122-148.
9. Epigraphica Indica, XX 1929-30, p. 18.
10. Ibid., pp. 18-19.
11. Ibid., p. 19.
12. Ibid., p. 19.
13. Ibid., p. 17.
14. Ibid., p. 20.
15. Ibid., p. 21.
16. Ibid., pp. 21-22.
17. Archaeological Survey of South India, 1887, pp. 100 ff.
18. Epigraphica Indica, XXI, p. 62.
19. Epigraphica Indica, XX, p. 23.

20. Ibid. p. 24.
21. Cambridge History of India, p. 333.
22. Epigraphica Indica, XVII, 1923-24, p. 329.
23. The Ten Points of Dispute were:

    (1) Practice of carrying salt in a horn. (2) Practice of taking meals after mid-day. (3) Practice of going to another village and taking a second meal there on the same day. (4) Observance of ceremonies in various places in the same parish (Monastery). (5) Practice of obtaining sanction for a deed after it was done. (6) Use of customs as precedents. (7) Drinking of butter milk after meals. (8) The drinking of toddy. (9) Use of borderless sheets. (10) Acceptance of gold and silver.
24. The seven sub-sects in the Mahasanghika group were:

    Ekavyavaharika, Caityika (Caityaka), Kakuttika (gokulika); Bahusrutiya, Prajnaptivada, Purvasaila and Aparasaila. The sub-sects in the Theravada group were : Mahasasaka, Vatisputriya, Sammittya, Sannagarika, Bhadrayaniya, Dharmottariya, Sarvastivada, Dharmaguptika, Kasyapiya, Haimavata and Samkrantika.
25. Nalinaksha Dutt, Buddhist Sects in India. Delhi, 1977, pp. 68-69.
26. C. Sivaramaurti, Bulletin of the Madras Government Museum, Amaravati Sculptures in the Madras Museum. New Series-General Section, Vol. IV, Madras, 1977, p. 16.
27. Thomas Watters. On Yuan Chwang's Travels in India, Vol. II, p. 203.
28. E.R.E. No. VIII, p. 235.
29. L.M. Joshi, Life and Times of the Madhyamika Philosopher Nagarjuna, The Maha Bodhi, Vol. 73, No.2, February 1965, p. 42.
30. K. Venkata Ramanan, Nagarjuna's Philosophy As Presented In The Maha-Prajnaparamita-Sastra, 1971, Introduction, p. 27.
31. P.V. Bapat, Edited, 2500 Years of Buddhism, Delhi, 1956, p. 120.
32. Golden Zephyr - Instructions from Spiritual Friend - Nagarjuna and Lama Mipham, Translated from the Tibetan by Leslie Kawamura, Dharma Publishing, 1975, pp. 114-116.

33. Nagarjuna is said to have lived a very long life, as long as 300 years or even 600 years, according to Tibetan sources. After analysing all relevant sources, L.M. Joshi assigns Nagarjuna a life of about 200 years, from 30 B.C. to 130 A.C. Cf. The Maha Bodhi, Volume 73, February 1965, pp. 42-47.
34. Bhikshu Sangharakshita, A Survey of Buddhism, Bangalore, 1965, p. 348.
35. Ibid. p. 345.
36. Ref. Friendrick V. Lustig (Ashin Ananda), The Maha Bodhi July-August 1976, p. 266.
37. Epigraphica Indica, XX 1929-30, p. 22.
38. D.C. Sircar and A.N. Lahiri - Epigraphica Indica, Vol. XXXIII p. 250. Also see M.D. Khare, Ceylonese Monks in Nagarjuna-konda, The Maha Bodhi, December 1964, pp. 317-19.
39. Samuel Beal, SI-YU-KI Buddhist Records of the Western World, Delhi, 1981 Reprint, Vol. II, p. 221.
40. H. Sarkar, and S.P. Nainar, Amaravati, Archaeological Survey of India, New Delhi, 1980, p. 9.
41. The relics in the Amaravati Museum are described here largely in the words of H. Sarkar and S.P. Nainar, Amaravati, Archaeological Survey of India, New Delhi, 1980.
42. C. Sivaramamurti, Amaravati Sculptures in the Government Museum, Madras, 1977, pp. 151-270.
43. Ibid., Inscriptions, pp. 271-304.
44. Ibid. For illustration, we quote here five inscriptions in full:
    (1) Success! This upright slab is the pious gift of Pesama the medicant monk residing at Mahavanasela, the pupil at the feet of the great elder (mahathera) Parivinuta living at Pusakavana and scholar in Samyutaka bhana (i.e. Samyutta Nikaya) and of Hamgha (Sangha). (No. 34, p. 279).
    (2) Success! Meritorious gift of a slab with an overflowing vase by the leather-worker (camakara) Vidhika, the son of the teacher Naga, with his mother, his wife, his brothers, his son Naga, his daughters and with his jnatis, friends and relations. (No. 41, p. 281).

(3) Adoration to Siddharta (Siddhartha) : Gift of coping stone to the great stupa of the Lord by the wife of the merchant Samuda (Samudra), the son of the householder Hangha (Sangha), living in the chief city of the Puki district, and by the ... house (holder) Kotacadi, for the welfare and happiness of the whole world. (No. 102, p. 298).

(4) Success! Adoration to the Lord Buddha, the best of all beings! (Gift) of the sister of the monk (pavaita), living at Mandara. (No. 10, p. 300).

(5) Success! At the foot of the great caitya of the Lord has been placed a lamp pillar, as seat of merit, by Khada (Skanda), the wife of the householder Sidhata (Sidhartha) of the Jadikiya (Caityaka) school, with daughters, sons, mother, brothers, daughters-in-law of the house ..... and her own jnatis (husband's paternal cousins). (No. 118, p. 302).

45. The great archaeologist, A.H. Longhurst, in The Buddhist Antiquities of Nagarjunakonda (1938) says "The ruthless manner in which all the buildings at Nagarjuna Konda have been destroyed is simply appalling and cannot represent the work of treasure-seekers alone as so many of the pillars, statues and sculptures have been wantonly smashed to pieces. Local tradition relates that the great Hindu philosopher and preacher Shankaracharya of medieval time came to Nagarjuna Konda with a host of followers and destroyed the Buddhist monuments".

46. The exhibits in the Nagarjunakonda Museum are described largely on the basis of the guide on Nagarjunakonda by H. Sarkar and B.N. Misra published by the Archaeological Survey of India, New Delhi, 1980.

47. Archaeological Survey of South India, 1887, pp. 100ff.

48. Newstime, Hyderabad, 22 June, 1986.

49. K.R. Srinivasan, Temples of South India, New Delhi, 1979 edition, p. 24.

50. N. Ramesan, Temples and Legends of Andhra, p. 114.

51. I.K. Sarma, Studies in Early Buddhist Monuments and Brahmi inscriptions of Andhra Desa, Nagpur, 1988, p.9.

52. N. Ramesan, Temples and Legends of Andhra Desa, p. 14ff.
53. Ibid.
54. According to some scholars, Potalka was one of the early seats of Vajrayana Buddhism. L.M. Joshi (Studies in Buddhist Culture in India, New Delhi, 1967, pp. xx-xxi) says:

    ".... Potalka Parvata has been suggested as a third possible early seat of the origin of Vajrayana in the far south apart from Dhanyakataka and Sriparvata; this suggestion is based on the authority of Hsuan-tsang, the Sadhanamala and the Gilgit text of the Sarva-tathagata-dhisthanasattv-avalokanar-Buddhaksetra-san-darsanavyuha. South Indian origin of Tantrika Buddhism, already suggested many years ago by the late Pt. Rahula Sankrityayana, has been further strengthened by fresh evidence extracted from the Sekoddeṣatika, the Blue Annals, the Biography of Dharmasvamin and the above mentioned Gilgit text. These authorities finally overthrow the generally accepted theory of Bengali origin of Tantrika Buddhism."
55. Please see discussion under 'Royal Patronage' in the chapter on Tamil Nadu.
56. Samuel Beal, Buddhist Records of the Western World, Delhi, 1981, Vol. II, p. 233.
57. A.R. Kulkarni, The Buddha The Trimurti and Modern Hinduism, Nagpur, 1980, pp. 22-23.
58. B. Seshagiiri Rao, Studies in South India Jainism, Delhi, 1982 edition, p. 80.

5

Karnataka

Following the reorganisation of Indian States on linguistic basis, the new Mysore State was formed on Ist November 1956. Seventeen years later, on Ist November, 1973, the Kannada speaking State was renamed as Karnataka. The area of Karnataka is 191773 sq. kilometres, and Bangalore, the city of gardens, is its capital.

(I) ROYAL PATRONAGE

A major part of modern day Karnataka was part of the Mauryan Empire right from the time of Chandragupta Maurya. However, the recently discovered Asokan rock edict at Sannati in Gulbarga district indicates that Asoka may have annexed northern part of Karnataka, alongwith Kalinga. Whatever may be the case, the fact remains that Asoka had made Karnataka a major centre of his *Dhamma-Vijaya* campaign. The discovery of as many as nine rock edicts of Asoka in Karnataka confirms this view. These rock edicts are at Maski, Gavimath, Palkigundu and Koppal in Raichur district; Brahmagiri, Siddapura and Jaitingarameshwara in Chitradurga district; and Nittur and Udegolam in Bellary district. Besides these edicts, Asoka had also specifically deputed two monk-missionaries to preach and propagate the *Dhamma* in Karnataka. Thus, Buddhism had taken roots in Karnataka during the reign of Asoka.

After the decline of the Mauryan rule, the Satavahanas rose to power in Deccan. A portion of Karnataka formed part of their kingdom which covered parts of Andhra and Maharashtra as well. The Satavahanas, who ruled for over 450 years (from second century BC to second century AD) patronised Buddhism for cultural reasons. It was during the Satavahana rule that the Deccan saw one of the greatest efflorscence of art and culture. Most of the Buddhist caves in Western Deccan (Maharashtra) as well as the Buddhist monuments in Eastern Deccan (Andhra) were created during the Satavahana period. Similar thing may have happened in the adjoining parts of Karnataka. It is significant that the largest Rock-cut Buddhist Temple at Karla (Karle), near Lonavla in Maharashtra, excavated some time in the first century BC, was the gift of a devout Buddhist merchant of Vanavasi or Vaijayanti, a city said to be on the bank of the river Varada in North Kanara district of Karnataka. An inscription in the cave itself says:[1] "Seth Bhutapala from Vaijayanti has established a rock mansion-the most excellent in Jambudvipa (India)."

With the downfall of the Satavahanas, Buddhism appears to have yielded ground to Jainism in Karnataka. As we know, Buddhism was patronised by most of the Kings, Princes and the people of North India. In contrast, Jainism appears to have faired much better in South India, that is, the areas outside the influence of early Buddhism. The glorious age of Jainism in South India in general, and in Karnataka in particular, was under the Ganga Kings who rose to power in the fourth century AD, and made Jainism the state religion. Even so, the Ganga kings were tolerent, and Madhava II (540-565 AD) gave grants[2] to Buddhism too. The two other dynasties that ruled Karnataka after the Ganga kings were the Western Chalukyas (550-747 AD) and the Rashtrakutas (798-912 AD) were also non-Buddhists. Notwithstanding the lack of royal patronage, Buddhism managed to survive in certain pockets of Karnataka as late as the twelfth century AD.

(II) BUDDHIST SAINTS AND SCHOLARS

The first two Buddhist monks to preach the *Dhamma* in Karnataka were Mahadeva and Rakkhita, the two missionaries deputed by Asoka after the Third Buddhist Council at Pataliputra. These monk-missionaries were stationed at Mahasiamandala (Mysore) and Vanavasi (North Kanara district) respectively. Besides these two pioneer monks, Aravana Adigal, the well-known preceptor of Manimekhalai, who was active in the Pandya, Chola and Chera kingdoms in the second century AD, may also have visited Karnataka in the course of his preaching tours. And even Nagarjuna, the famous Madhyamika teacher who flourished in the second century AD, may have also been associated with Karnataka. It is rather unfortunate that the names of the local Buddhist monks have not survived but there must have been many sons of the soil as Buddhism was prevalent in Karnataka for nearly 1500 years, from the third century BC onward.

(III) BUDDHIST SITES AND SHRINES

The most significant Buddhist relics in Karnataka have been discovered at Aiholi, Badami, Banabasi (Vanavasi) and Dambal.

I. Aiholi

The Buddhist *Chaitya* located on the Meguti hill at Aiholi is the most important surviving Buddhist temple in Karnataka. It was first of all identified as a Buddhist shrine by S. Settar. Following the lead given by Settar, S. Rajasekhara has further studied the structure thoroughly, and he, in his latest book 'Early Chalukya Art at Aiholi' gives a detailed description of the shrine as well as the sculptures and minature reliefs found in and around the Meguti Buddhist shrine.[3]

The *Chaitya* at Aiholi is a double storey structure, which is half structural and half excavated in rock. Its upper storey has a sanctum-sanctorum and a rectangular verandah which measures 8.78 metres by 2.15 metres. In the centre of the ceiling of the verandah there is a relief of the Buddha in preaching posture. The lower *chaitya* is also partly rock-cut and partly built. It has a shrine room with side cells, an ante-chamber and rectangular verandah. The ceiling of the ante-chamber is of uneven rock but the door is elaborately carved with reliefs depicting incidents from the life of the Buddha. Similarly, the door of the central shrine room is also finely carved with reliefs depicting Jataka tales and incidents from the life of the Buddha. The *chaitya* appears to be the oldest structure at Aiholi and is datable to the first half of the sixth century AD.

The best preserved sculpture at Aihole is on the ceiling of the upper storey of the chaitya. Says S. Rajasekhara[4]:

"On the ceiling of the upper storey of the *chaitya* is the best preserved of the three sculptures of the Buddha found at Aihole. In this relief the Buddha is seated on the *padmapitha* in the *satvaparyankasana*. His right hand is placed against the chest in the *Vyakhyana mudra*, while the left is placed on the sole of the right foot with the palm facing upwards. he is partly draped. The right shoulder and a part of the right breast are left uncovered. Above the head is a triple umbrella. He is flanked by attendants. The sculpture of the Buddha on the ceiling measures about 61 cm in height."

A number of minature reliefs found on the door jambs of the sanctum and the *antarala* of the lower structure of the chaitya are badly demaged or badly worn out. Among the the seven tolerably intact reliefs, three relate to the incidents from Buddha's life.[5] These are 'the Great Departure' wherein Siddhartha leaves the home to seek enlightenment; Buddha's First Sermon at Sarnath; and Devadatta's attempts to kill the Buddha-first by releasing a rouge elephant on the road on which the Buddha was coming in Rajgir, and again by throwing a big boulder from height to crush the Buddha. This also happened at Rajgir (ancient Rajagaha). The other surviving reliefs depict four Jatakas: the *Culla-hamsa Jataka, Aramadusaka Jataka, Surpana Jataka,* and *Vessantara Jataka.*

A mutilated headless Buddha image kept outside the chaitya is also about 61 cm in height. yet another Buddha image (now in the museum at Aiholi) shows the Buddha seated on a *pitha,* rectangular cushion. Unlike the other two, this image is cut in granite. The robe worn by the Buddha is clearly carved. There is also a huge Bodhisattva image near the entrance to the Meguti hill.

2. Badami

Badami, the capital city of the Chalukyans, in the sixth century AD, was also associated with Buddhism. The Buddhist relics[6] here have survived in the shape of a Buddhist Cave datable to the sixth century AD. There is also a figure, identified as Padmapani, the Bodhisattva, of the same period.

3. Dambal

Dambal in the Dharwar district was a Buddhist centre as late as the 12th century AD. According to an inscription[7] of 1017 (1095AD), a temple of the Buddhist deity, *Tara*, and a Buddha *Vihara* were built there by the sixteen settis (sethis or merchants) of Dambal during the reign of Lakshmidevi, the queen of Vikramaditya VI. Another temple of *Tara* built at Dambal was by Sethi Sangaramaya of Lokkigundi.

4. Vanavasi

The capital city of the Kadambas, Vanavasi, also known as Vaijyanti, was one of the most prominent centres of Buddhism in Karnataka. When Hiuen Tsang, the Chinese pilgrim, visited this city in the seventh century AD, he saw there two sangharamas and three stupas. He says[8]:

"By the side of the royal palace is a great *sangharama* with some 300 priests, who are all men of distinction. This convent has a great vihara, a hundred feet and more in height. In it is a precious tiara, belonging to Sarvarthasiddha the prince. It is somewhat less than two feet in height, and is ornamented with gems and precious stones. it is kept in a jewelled casket."

"By the side of the city is a great *sangharama* in which is a *vihara* about 50 feet high. In this is a figure of Maitreya Bodhisattva carved out of Sandal-wood. It is about ten feet high. It is the work of the Arhat Srutavimsatikoti."

The recent excavations on the site of Vanavasi or Banavasi have brought to light the remains of a Buddhist stupa. Commenting on this discovery, H.D. Sankalia says[9]:

"If this Banavasi can be excavated horizontally, it would give a good idea of Satavahana-Kadamba city. Even the small sporadic excavations, during the last 10 years, have laid bare the remains of a large apsidal structure, which does not seem to be an ordinary apsidal temple, but the remains of a Buddhist *stupa* planned like a *dharmachakra*. This becomes clear when we compare the photograph of the Banavasi structure with the *stupa* unearthed in 1971-72 at Sanghol, district Ludhiana, Punjab, Whereas in the former, only one radiating spoke of the wheel is seen (or has been exposed) in the latter, two broadly spaced, wide areas are pierced by five radiating spokes".

(IV) THE BUDDHIST LEGACY

As elsewhere in India, so also in Karnataka, a number of Buddha Viharas were converted and put to Hindu use. A beginning in this direction appears to have been made by Sankaracarya, the Vedanta teacher, who flourished in the early part of the ninth century. He is said to have founded his Sringeri Math in Chikmaglur district on the site of a Buddhist monastery. Another Buddhist shrine converted by the Hindus in Karnataka is the Shiva temple known as Kadri-Manjunatha in Mangalore district. According to M.G. Pai, Kadri-Majunatha was originally a Buddhist shrine and was known as 'Kadiraka *Vihara*'. Supporting the view of Pai, P.S. Jaini says[10]:

"In the suburbs of Mangalore, a city in southern Karnataka, stands a Saivite temple known as Kadri-Manjunatha, "Manjunatha" designates the *Siva-linga* enshrined therein. Now, although Siva is commonly referred to by titles terminating in "Natha" (e.g. Somanatha, Omkaranatha, Kedaranatha, Visvanatha, this particular name "Manjunatha" is *nowhere else* attested as a proper epithet of the god. Intrigued by this strange fact, Pai undertook to workout a chronological history of the temple in question. He found, first of all, that it had once been a Buddhist monastery and temple called Kadarika-vihara, within the shrine room stands an image of the Buddha. More important, from our point of view, is the additional presence therein of the beautiful bronze image of the *Bodhisattva* Avalokitesvara, also called Lokesvara. An inscription at the base of the Lokesvara image credits its establishment to one king Kundavarma of the Alupa dynasty, stating that "Kundavarma, the Alupa king, a great devotee of *Balacandraei-Khamani* (he who has the crescent moon as his crest-Jewel, i.e. Siva), consecrated the image of Lord Lokesvara in this pleasant *vihara* called Kadarika, four thousand one hundred and sixty-eight years after Kaliyuga" (i.e. 1068 A.D.). The interesting point here is that an image of Lokesvara should have been erected in a Buddhist temple by king who was devoted to Siva. Clearly it was not the Buddha who was being worshipped, but a *Bodhisattva* who had in some way been *integrated with Siva.*

Pai has shown, further, that Lokasvara was identified with Matsyendranatha, a Saivite saint said to have become divine by attaining oneness with Sakti. Numerous caves in the vicinity of Kadri are dedicated to ascetics of the Natha order which this saint established, and an image of Matsyendranatha himself (identified by the mark of a fish) adorns the outer wall of the "Kadarika-vihara" temple. Considering the name "Manjunatha" in light of all this information, Pai concluded that the *vihara* was originally a centre of the cult of the *Bodhisattva* Manjusri. At a latter time, when this and other heavenly *bodhisattvas* had become identified with Saivite deities, Natha ascetics established a *Siva-linga* in the temple and called it by the present name. Still later, disciples of Matsyendranatha, among whom should be included king Kundavarma, arranged for the placing of the extant Lokesvara image, an image representing what they have regarded as the divine form of their master.

The worship of the *Siva-linga* and its associated *bodhi-sattva* no doubt continued for several centuries, until what had originally been a Buddhist center was converted into a purely Saivite temple."

Similar transformation may have taken place at other places also.

The Buddhist legacy in Karnataka survives in a much more pronounced manner in the teachings of Basavesara or Basava, a religious teacher who flourished in the 12th century. Born in about 1105 AD in an orthodox Brahmin family at Bagewadi in Bijapur district, Basava rose to a high position of royal Treasurer of the then Chalukyan kingdom. Basava was a deeply religious person and a social reformer too. Not satisfied with the brahmanical society, he rebelled against the orthodoxy, and went on to establish his own sect, now known as Virasaivism. The follower of this faith is a sworn votary of Siva, and worship of *Ishta-Linga* is the essential part of Virasaivism. But here ends the Hindu element as the teachings of Basava are primarily based on the teachings of the Buddha. K.R. Basavaraja has summed up Basava's teachings as follows:[11]

"This new faith is a departure from the labyrinth of mechanical rituals of the Vedic tradition in essentials. In this faith there is no place for the scared fire and the sacrificial rituals. And social gradation such as Brahmana, Sudra, and the four fold *asrama* scheme of life are not accepted. The sacraments and rituals are reduced to the minimum, the most essential being only three, initiation, marriage and funeral. The soul, being pure, is free from physical pollutions. The goal of human life is the union of the individual soul with the Supreme. This can be achieved by the rules of *Ashtavarana*, the eight-fold covering of spiritual aids, which is the means for developing one's individuality; the *Panchachara* or the five-fold conduct which elevates the individual in his social environment; and *Shasthala*, the six-fold stage which leads him on the path of spiritual progress and perfection. Among the *Ashtavarana*, the triad, the *Guru* (the spiritual guide), the *Linga* (the mystic emblem of the Supreme) and the *Jangama* (the itinerant minister of religion and morality) occupy a prominent place. Thus, this religion is free from the shortcomings like the rituals, superstitions and distinctions based on caste, creed and sex."

As is evident from the above summary of Basava's teachings, the founder of Virasaivism had in fact modelled his *Ashtavarana*, the eight-fold covering or spiritual aids, on the Buddhist Eightfold path (*astanga marga* or *atthnagika magga* in Pali); the *Panchachara* or the five-fold conduct which elevates the individual, on the Five Moral Precepts (*panca sila*); and *Shasthala*, the six-fold stage which leads him on the path of spiritual progress and perfection, on the six Higher Powers or Supernatural Knowledges (*abhijnas* or *abhinnas* in Pali) taught by the Buddha. Further, among the *Ashtavarana*, the triad, the *Guru*, the *Linga*, and *Jangama* is almost a replica of the Buddhist Triple-Gem: the *Buddha*, the *Dhamma* and the *Sangha*. In other words, Virasaivism is Saivism in theory and Buddhism in practice.

(V) THE REVIVAL MOVEMENT

The revival of Buddhism in Karnataka, as in Tamil Nadu, was pioneereed by the South India Buddhist Association, Madras which was founded by Pandit Ayoti Dasa (Ayodhya Dasa) in 1900. As a result of the missionary zeal of Appadorai or Appaswamy, who came to the Kolar Gold Fields (KG.F.) along with Tamil labourers, Buddhism took strong roots in K.G.F. The Buddha Vihara at Champion Reef is the most important Buddhist temple in the Kolar Gold Fields.

The South India Buddhist Association was followed by the Maha Bodhi Society of India which founded a Buddha Vihara in Bangalore, the capital of modern Karnataka. This Vihara at 14, Kalidasa Road, Gandhinagar, Bangalore, is now the chief centre of Buddhism in Karnataka. Though founded in 1940 on a plot of land given free by the then Government of Mysore, it became a living centre of Buddhism only in 1956 after the arrival of Acharya Buddharakkhita. Venerable Buddharakkhita, born in 1922, became a Buddhist monk in the early 1950's after resigning his post of an engineer in the British Army. He worked for sometime at the Nalanda Mahavihara, and had a thorough training under qualified masters in India and Sri Lanka. As a result of his single-minded devotion and dedication, the Maha Bodhi Society, Bangalore is now a flourishing Buddhist centre. It has an Institute of Buddhology, an International Meditation Centre, a Stupa and Printing Press. Some other organisations founded by Acharya Buddharkkhita are: Mahabodhi Maitri Mandal, Bangalore and Mysore; Mahabodhi Arogya Hospital and Artificial Limb Centre, Bangalore; and Mahabodhi Vidyapeth, Bangalore with Branches at Mysore. Ven. Buddharakkhita is now a well-known meditator, psychologist, philosopher and educationist. He is also a prolific writer, and has published over fifty books and pamphlets on Buddha-Dhamma in English, Pali and Kannada. He is also the editor of the monthly journal 'Dhamma' which was founded by him in 1976. The multifarious activities of the Maha Bodhi Society, Bangalore are now being looked after by Ven. Bhikkhu Sanghasena and Bhikkhu Ananda.

Dr. B.R. Ambedkar, the greatest Pioneer of Buddhist Revival in India, had planned to construct a magnificent Buddhist Seminary for the training of Buddhist monks and nuns on a plot of land graciously donated for this purpose by the Maharaja of Mysore. Due to the sudden demise of Dr. Ambedkar, this project could not be accomplished. However, the project has been now taken up by the Buddha Dhamma Chakra Parivarthana Samithi, Buddha Bhoomi, Rajamhalvilas Extension, Bangalore under the able guidance of B. Basavalingappa, Minister for Science and Technology, Government of Karnataka.

The important Buddha *Vihara* in Mysore city is the Ashoka *Vihara* in Ashokapuram.

As per 1981 Census, there are 42,147 Buddhists in Karnataka. The Tibetans, who migrated to India in 1959 in the wake of the Chinese invasion, form a substantial portion of the Buddhist population in the State. The four Tibetan settlements in Karnataka are at Bylakuppe (near Mysore), Mundgod (in North Kanara district), Cauvery Valley, and Kollegal. The most important Tibetan Buddhist monasteries in Karnataka are : Thegchay Ling Tibetan Monastery, Bylakuppe, and Namgoling Tibetan Monastery, Bylakuppe.

Notes and References

1. J. Burgess, Archaeological Survey of India, Volume IV, Report on the Buddhist Cave Temples And Their Inscriptions, London 1883, p.90.
2. B. Vasantha Shetty, Studies in Karnataka History, New Delhi, 1984, p.28.
3. S. Rajasekhara, Early Chalukyan Art at Aiholi, New Delhi, 1985, pp. 184-88.
4. IIbid., p. 185.
5. Ibid., pp. 186-187.
6. B. Vasantha Shetty, Studies in Karnataka History, New Delhi, 1984, pp. 37-38.
7. Ed. P.V. Bapat, 2500 years of Buddhism, 1987 edition, p. 293.
8. Samuel Beal, SI-YU Ki, Buddhist Records of the Western World, Translated from the Chinese of Hiuen Tsiang, Two Volumes, Reprint, Delhi, 1981 edition, Vol. II, p. 254.
9. H.D. Sankalia, Indian Achaeology Today, p. 143.
10. Padmanabh S. Jaini, The Disappearance of Buddhism and The Survival of Jainism: A Study in Contrast. Cf. Studies in History of Buddhism, Ed. A.K. Narain, Delhi, 1976, p.87.
11. K.R. Basavaraja, Basavesara - His Life and Contributions. Cf. A Pranorama of Indian Culture (Professor A Sreedhara Menon Felicitation Volume), Edited by K.K. Kusuman, New Delhi, 1990, p. 310.

6

Kerala

The present day Malayalam speaking Kerala State came into existence on First November, 1956, with the amalgamation of Malabar with the Travancore and Cochin States, consequent upon the reorganisation of Indian States on linguistic basis. Occupying a narrow strip of land on the West Coast, Kerala is one of the smallest States of India; its area being only 38,864 sq. kilometers. Trivandrum is the capital of Kerala.

(I) ROYAL PATRONAGE

Though Kerala lay outside the Mauryan Empire, yet it seems certain that Buddhism came firmly to this tiny State during Asoka's reign (273-232 BC). In his second major rock edict found at Girnar, Asoka refers to the rulers of this land as Keralputras living on his frontiers. The Girnar edict further tells us that Asoka had established hospitals for men and beasts in Kerala. This would obviously imply that the Buddhist missionaries deputed by Asoka to the southern region were active in Kerala too. That it was so, is confirmed by the events in the following centuries.

According to the traditional history of Chera Desa or Kerala, the first Buddhist ruler of Kerala was Jayasimha Perumal, the ruler of Quilon in Travancore in the first century BC. The most important Buddhist king of Kerala was Bana Permual who flourished towards the closing years of the third century AD. He was popularly known as Baudha Perumal.[1] Some of the other Chera kings also patronised Buddhism. The capital of the Chera kings was Vanji or Vanchi, now known as Karur, adjacent to Cranganur, on the bank of the river Periyar, about 30 miles north of Cochin.

Another important Buddhist ruler of Kerala was King Vikramaditya Varagunan.[2] He ruled central part of Kerala in the ninth century A.D. His capital was Srimulavasam near modern Alwaye. The rulers of Srimulavasam were known as Mushaka Kings. An ancient Sanskrit work called *Mushaka Vamsa* gives a vivid description of the city and the rulers of Srimulavasm. According to this work, there were many Buddhist shrines and monasteries in the city. King Varagunan propagated Buddhism not only in South India but also in other parts of India. Prof. Foucher had discovered a Buddhist image at Kandhar on which he found the following inscription: "*Dakshinapathe Mulavamasa Lokanatha*" or the Ruler of Srimulavasam in South India. It amply proves the missionary activities of King Varagunan who had sent this image to Kandhar. This king also donated lands and other valuables for the maintenance and construction of Buddhist shrines in Kerala.

One of the cardinal causes which hastened the decline of and downfall of Buddhism in India was its persecution at the hands of the rulers as well as religious fanatics. Such a thing seems to have happened in an organised manner in Kerala. According to *Keralotpatti*, a 17th century chronicle in Malayalam, the Kerala Buddhists were subjected to severe persecution by the Brahmins atleast on two occasions. The first persecution followed the conversion of Bana Perumal in the third century AD. As the Brahmins were opposed to his conversion, "Perumal was dethroned and the Buddhists had their tongues cut out and then expelled from the country".[3] Next time the Buddhists or Bauddhas of Malabar were persecuted following their confutation by Kamarila Bhatta in the eighth century AD. Kumarila Bhatta not only preached against the Buddhists, but also instigated thc king to persecute them. The ruthless persecution of the Buddhists by Suddhanvan, at the instigation Kumarila Bhatta, is also recorded in two biographies of Sankaracarya, that is, the Sankara-Viajay by Anandagiri, a direct disciple of Sankaracarya, and Sankara-digvijayam by Madhava (14th century AD). In fact, Madhava Acharya asserts that, at the instigation of Kumarila Bhatta, Suddhanvan commanded his servants to put to death the old men and the children of the Buddhists from Kanya Kumari to the Himalaya. He further ordered that let him who slays not, be slain;[4]

"A-secor-a tushadre tu Bauddhanam vriddabalakan na hantityahsahantavyo bhrityan intyanwasad nripah"

"The king commanded his servants to put to death the old men and the children of the Bauddhas from the southern most point of India to the snowy mountain; let him who slays not, by slain."[5]

Kumarila Bhatta was followed by another avowed enemy of Buddhism. He was Sankara, a Nambudiri Brahmin, born at Kaladi, near Cochin in Kerala, in 788 A.D. Sankara is credited with worsting the Buddhist priests in Malabar and other places in India. He is one of the Hindu teachers held responsible for the persecution of Buddhists. In fact, he struck a terror into the hearts of the Buddhists. According to a Tibetan tradition, at his approach, "the Buddhists in the monasteries began to disappear pell-mell".[6]

(II) BUDDHIST SAINTS AND SCHOLARS

The *Silappadikaram* and the *Manimekhalai,* the two ancient classics in the Tamil language, give us glimpses of Buddhism in ancient Kerala, the Chera Desa. The *Silappadikaram* (The Book of the Anklet), the first Tamil epic, was written by Ilango-Adigal, a Jaina ascetic and brother of the Chera monarch, Senguttuvan, who flourished in the second century AD. This epic tells the story of Kovalan, a rich merchant of Kaveripattinam or Puhar who fell in love with Madhavi, a dancing girl. According to *Silappadikaram,* its hero and heroine, Kovalan and Kannaki, were Buddhists. The

Manimekhalai tells the story of Madhavi and Manimekhalai, the daughter of Kovalan and Madhavi, who later became a Buddhist nun. The *Manimekhalai* was composed by Sittalai Sattanar, the greatest Buddhist poet, who was contemporary of Ilango - Adigal. In the epic *Manimekhalai* it is mentioned that the great grandfather of Kovalan had built a Buddhist shrine[7] at Vanji or Vanchi, the Chera capital. Kovalan's grandfather is said to have been won over to Buddhism by a Bhikkhu living in a place named Padapanka Jamalaya. Thus the capital of the Chera kings, Vanji, had been associated with notable Buddhist saints from the earliest times. It was to this city that Aravan Adigal, the noted Buddhist missionary and the preceptor of Manimekhalai, and several other noted Buddhists, had first migrated from Kaveripattinam and propagated the *Dhamma* in Kerala. As a result of their efforts, Buddhism endured for long in Kerala. Unfortunately, the names of the Buddhist savants, who preached and propagated the Buddha-Dhamma through the ages till its final eclipse after the ninth century AD, have not survived. But it seems plausible that Kerala was by and large looked after by the Buddhist saints and scholars who lived at Kanchipuram in the present day Tamil Nadu.

(III) BUDDHIST SITES AND SHRINES

Buddhism flourished most in ancient Kerala in the area which comprises the present day Alleppey and Quilon districts. The discovery of a large number of Buddha images from this area has confirmed this fact. The most notable Buddha image is that of the famous Karumadikuttan near Ambalapuzha. The most notable Buddhist shrine Srimulavasam, the capital city of King Vikramaditya Varagunan (885-925 AD) has been located by the scholars in the region between Ambalapuzha and Trikkunnapuzha in Alleppey district. Among the Buddhist temples appropriated by the Hindus, prominent ones are the Vadakkunathan temple, Trichur[8] and the Siva temple at Madavoorpara in Kazhakuttam near Trivandrum. Further, "the names of the places in Central Travancore where the images of Buddha were discovered incorporate the word *"palli"*, either as suffix or prefix, *"Ezhu-thu-palli"* and *"Palli-koodam"*, the Malayalam equivalents of "school" also have the word *"palli"* as suffix or prefix. The landed properties assigned to Buddhist shrines are referred to as *"Palli-puram"* and *"Pali-chantham"* in ancient documents. The word *"palli"* is said to have been the ancient name for a Buddhist shrine in Kerala. Historians are therefore led to the conjecture that the places in Kerala, which have the word *"palli"*, either as suffix or prefix like Karnagapally, Karthigapally, Kanjirapally, Edappally, Talapally, Mallapally, Mynagappally, Chandanappally, Anandappally, Vendarappally, Vazhappally, Pathirappally, Mothapalliyur, Pallipuram Pallikkunnu, Pallathuruthy, Palluruthy, Pallickal etc. were once the seats of Buddhist shrines".[9]

The Buddhist relics in Kerala also include several sculptural caves[10] and umbrella-stones at various places in Malabar, and Cochin area. Generally, these caves are designed to serve as living accommodation for the Buddhist monks but some of them were excavated merely to deposit the bodily relics of the venerable Buddhist monks. In Malabar, two caves are at Kanjiramcode (two miles to the north-east of Thaliparamba), six caves at Keezhariyur (three miles to the north-east of Quilon), one cave at Dharmadam or Dharmapattanam (four miles to the north of Tellecherry) and one cave at Feroke, near the railway station. In the Cochin area, such caves are seen at Kakkad, Cjowannur, Arikanniyur, Eyyal and Kattakampally in Talapally taluk. There are also half a dozen umbrella-stones[11] at Arikaniyur and more than two dozen at Cherumanangad in Talapally taluk.

(IV) THE BUDDHIST LEGACY

Buddhism has left a deep mark on the life and culture of the people of Kerala. In order to woo the masses to Hinduism, the Brahmins not only adopted the popular Buddhist customs and manners in their system but they also inducted Lord Buddha in the Hindu pantheon under the name of *Dharma Sasta* or *Ayyappa*. That *Sasta* is none else but the Buddha has been accepted by many scholars. According to T.A. Gopinatha Rao[12]:

"This deity is called Shasta because he is able to control and rule over the whole world; etymologically therefore the word means a ruler of a country; and is sometimes applied to teachers and fathers. The Amarkosha applies the name to Buddha also. The Tamil Nighantus call him by the additional names of Satavahana, the rider of the white elephant, Kari, the wielder of the weapon known as sendu, the consort of Purana and Pushkala, the protector of Dharma and Yogi; they also state that the vehicle of *Sasta* is the elephant and the crest of his banner a cock. The names, rider of the white elephant, Yogi, protector of Dharma coupled with the significance of Buddha applied to *Sasta* in the *Amarkosha* incline one to conclude that Buddha as conceived and worshiped in the Tamil country was ultimately included in the Hindu Patheon and a Puranic story invented for his origin at a later period of the history of Hindu Iconology..."

And what is the story invented by the Brahmins? To quote the words of K.R. Vaidyanathan[13]:

"The story is that, Siva was captivated by the charms of Mohini in which form Vishnu appeared at the time of churning of the Ocean of Milk in order to entice the asuras so that the devas could divide the nectar among themselves. Siva succumbed to the beauty of Mohini and Sasta is believed to have been born out of the union".

Tracing the history of this mythical story, T.A. Gopinatha Rao says[14]:

"This deity which is very peculiar to the Dravida country does not appear to have been known to to the region north of Godavari. In no early Sanskrit work is the deity mentioned. Even the dictionaries do not record this name and give its origin...."

In the Vishnu Purana, we hear about Mohini, but......" It is in the Shri Bhagwata that we learn for the first time that Hara fell in love with Vishnu in his form of Mohini. From the union between Hara and Hari, Arya, Shasta or Hariharputra is said to have been born..."

"..... The Suprabhedagama very distinctly mentions that Sasta was born of Mohini, the form assumed by Vishnu for the purpose of distributing the amrita among the gods when it was churned from the milk ocean, by the union with her of Hara...."

In the present day Kerala, *Sastha* as a minor deity is seen within the precincts of almost all the Hindu temples but there are also some major temples dedicated to Sastha. Significantly enough, all such *Sastha* temples, in accordance with the Buddhist practice of locating the monasteries in isolated places, are located in deep forests or inaccessible mountain tops, such as, Achenkoil, Aryankavu, Kulathamcotta, Kulathupuzha and Sabrarimala.[15] Some other important *Sastha* shrines are : Chalat (Cannanore), Devikulam, Erumeli, Karikode, Kumarakam, Omallur, Pandalam, Perumbavaboor, Punjar, Takazhi, Trikunnapuzha and Tirunavai.

The Sabarimala temple is the most famous and popular Sasta or Ayyappa shrine in Kerala. The practices associated with this shrine make it amply clear that the Lord Ayyappa worshipped here is the Buddha.

Firstly, Sabarimala shrine is the only shrine in Kerala where no caste restrictions are observed. Like the Buddhist shrines, the Sabarimala shrine is open to all, irrespective of caste, creed, religion and social status. Here, the high and low, the rich and the poor, meet on equal terms; all are alike - Ayyappas, as the devotees are called after the deity itself.

Secondly, as says A. Sreedhara Menon[16], "The pilgrims to the Sastha shrine of Sabarimala observe strict vows of non-violence, vegetarianism and abstinence from worldly pleasures prior to the pilgrimage. This practice is in conformity with the Buddhist doctrine of *Ahimsa*. The pilgrims do not observe any caste distinctions during the period of their vow. The sing-song repitition of "*Saranam Ayyappa*" by the pilgrims reminds us of the triple *saranam* formula of the *Buddha*, the *Dharma*, and the *Sangha* of the Buddhists. Sastha is himself called Dharma Sastha."

Thirdly, the austerities observed by the devotees visiting the Sabarimala shrine are just an improvised version of the Eight Precepts (*Ashta Sila*) observed by the Buddhists on auspicious days, Full Moon day etc. The Buddhist Eight Precepts are : to abstain from killing, stealing, incelibacy, lying, intoxicants, taking food at unreasonable time, amusement shows, from the use of garlands, perfumes and from things that tend to beautify and adorn (the person), and lastly from (using) high and luxurious seats and beds.

In the light of the above evidence it can be safely assumed that the Sabarimala shrine was once a Buddhist shrine.

Not only the Buddhist shrines were appropriated by the Hindus in Kerala, even the images, processions, utsavas etc. were modelled after those of the Buddhists. K.R. Vaidyanathan says[17]:

"Like Jainism, Buddhsim also held sway in ancient Kerala during the reign of Ashoka in the 3rd century B.C. coming by sea, Buddhism was popular in coastal districts, Karumati, Mavelikkara, Bharanikkavu, Pallikkal, Karunagappalli, Idappalli, Dharmapattabnam, Matayi and Pallikkunnu being its chief centres.... Many prominent Hindu temples of today like the Vadakkunathan temple, Trichur and the Kurumba Bhagwati temple, Kondugallur, and even the famous Ayyappa shrine atop Sabarimala are believed to have been at one time Buddhist shrines.... While Jainism did hardly leave any impress on Kerala society, Buddhism was absorbed in Hinduism in respect of some of its ceremonies and forms of worship. The images, processions and *utsavam*, etc. associated, with popular worship in present day Hindu temples in Kerala are said to be a legacy of Buddhism. Even the *chakriya kuttu* conducted in temples is said to be an adaptation of the Buddhist monk's religious exposition."

One of the popular festivals in the Alleppey and Quilon districts of Kerala is Kutirakettu. This festivity resembles even in details with the car festival of the Buddhists. Describing this festival, Sreedhara Menon says[18] : "An important festivity associated, with temple festivals in the Quilon and Alleppey

Districts is the *Kettukazcha* or *Kutirakettu*. The main feature of the festival is that people from different *Karas* adjoining the temple concerned bring huge *rathams* or cars varying in height. The smaller ones are called *rathams* and the bigger one *kutira*. They are usually made of coconut wood or bamboo and decorated with white cloth and coloured silks. The *ratham* has several tiers which give it the appearance of the *gopuram* (tower) of a temple. The images of the Hindu gods and goddesses and effigies of Puranic figures like Bhima, Panchali, Hanuman, etc. are kept in the *ratham*. While the smaller ones are carried on shoulders, the bigger ones are drawn by the people on four wheels. The *rathams* coming from different *Karas* assemble on the four sides of the temple and they are taken in *Pradakshinam*. There is a view that the *Kettukazchacha* festival is a relic of Buddhism and that it resembles in its details with the Buddhist festival which Fahien, the Chinese pilgrim (5th century A.D.), wintessed at Pataliputra."

How exactly the temple festivals in Kerala resemble with the car procession wintessed by Fahien at Pataliputra (Patna) can be judged from the following account given by the Chinese pilgrim. He says[19], "Every year regularly on the eighth of the second moon they have a procession of images. They make a four-wheeled car of five storeys by lashing together bamboos; and on it there are crescent-headed javelins and partisans. It is more than 20 feet in height. It is like a pagoda in appearance, and draped round with a kind of cashmere which is painted in various colours. They make images of all the gods using gold, silver, and glass to ornament them, and suspending over them embroidered banners and canopies. At the four sides they make niches, each with a sitting Buddha inside and a *P'u-sa* (Bodhisattva) in attendance. There may be twenty cars, every one of which is differently decorated. On this day all the ecclesiastics and laymen in the district assemble, and occupy themselves with singing and rare music, burning incense and making offerings of flowers etc."

There is evidence to show that till the eighteenth century, there was a national festival known as Mamankam celebrated every twelve years in Kerala. Though the mode and scope of this festival changed with successive phases of history but according to some scholars, it arose as a grand celebration of the establishment of Buddhism[20] in Kerala. The traditional site of this festival was the bank of the Bharata River at Thrunava in North Kerala. Later on when Hinduism replaced Buddhism this festival was first transformed into a worship of the flagstaff of Indra (Indradhwaja Puja). Later, Vishnu replaced Indra.

According to V.R. Parameswaran Pillai[21]:

"In the *Keralotpatti* volumes, mention is made of a Pallivanavar who became a Buddhist. A tombstone to the north of the Nilampeur Bhagavati temple is supposed to contain the earthly remains of Pallivanavar, according to the belief of the people of that area. The location of the temple being called Pallipadikkal, the name of the *Devi* there being mentioned as Palliyil Bhagavati, the presence of a Buddha idol now being worshipped as Vishnu - all these in the aggregate lend weight to the presumption of Sri Sanku Iyer that this was an old Buddhist *vihara*. It may be similarly believed that Kilirur temple was also a Buddhist shrine."

To quote V.R.P. Pillai again[22]:

"Relics are still extant in many places of the remains of Buddha *viharas* known in the name of *Putharachhanmar*. Such place-names as Chakiankot Trppapur (Trppadapuram) Valukampara, Devendaranpotta near Marutvamala, Terur (Theras-Buddhists) village near Sucindram, Mahendragiri (Mahendra's momento sent by Asoka with Sangamitra for spreading the message of the Buddha in the southern country, etc.) are connected with the name of the Buddha."

Yet again[23]:

"*Talappoli, Kuttiyottam, Annamkettu,* etc., prevalent to this day in many temples are the relics of Buddhist customs. (*Annamkettu* is usual even in the present day in Burma festivals as in Kerala). The influence of the Buddhist religion is exemplified in such customs as the Onam festival, wearing of yellow clothes, restriction to vegetable food on holy days, idol worship etc."

The Bodhi Tree, sitting under which the Buddha attained supreme enlightenment, is the most sacred and revered tree for the Buddhists. The Bodhi Tree is revered even today in Kerala. And the Naga worship, which is widely prevalent in Kerala, is also said to be the legacy of Buddhism.

(V) THE REVIVAL MOVEMENT

The first pioneer Buddhist in modern Kerala was C. Krishnan, Editor of 'Mitavadi' published from Calicut. He was from the Ezhava caste and had embraced Buddhism in the early 1920's. On 9 February, 1925, he organised the first All Kerala Buddhist Conference which was inaugrated by M.R. Iyer and was presided over by C. Jinarajadasa. A Kerala Buddhist Association was formed at this Conference, with C. Krishnan as President. Two years later, on 16 May, 1927, a Buddha *Vihara* was opened at Calicut in a building at Paran Square donated by Krishnan. Ven. Dharmakhanda, who was the first Malayali to become a Buddhist monk, later joined hands with Krishnan and gave further impetus to the revival of Buddhism in Kerala.

At the request of C. Krishnan, the Maha Bodhi Society of India sent in August 1935 a Buddhist mission to Calicut under the leadership of Ven. Ananda Maitreya. The mission carried on a strenuous campaign, visited many towns, and addressed many meetings in the State. Same year, C. Krishnan who was now Member Legislative Council, was elected as President of the Malabar Branch of the Maha Bodhi Society. Through his generosity, the Maha Bodhi Society established in 1937 in Calicut the 'Maha Bodhi *Vihara*' to meet the needs of the growing number of Buddhists.

The revival movement has not been able to make much headway in this State. As per 1961 Census, there were only 228 Buddhists in Kerala; majority of them being in the Ernakulam district (143), followed by the Alleppey district (29). In 1981, the Buddhist population in Kerala was 223 only.

Notes and References

1. There is a concensus of opinion that Bana Perumal had embraced Buddhism. Keralotpathi (a Malayalam Chronical), Mangalore eidition, pp. 29-30m. (Keralavalisesha Mahatmayam (a Sanskrit work on the greatness of Kerala), p. 95; Mack : MSS.; Day's Land of Perumals, p. 365; Indian Antiquary, Vol. IIX, pp. 77-79, Note 4, Cf. History of Kerala, A.P. Padmanabha Menon, Vol. I, New Delhi 1982 edition, p. 445.
2. V.G. Nair, Heritage of Buddhism, (Buddhuism in South India), New Delhi, 1958, pp. 511-52.
3. K.P. Padmanabha Menon, History of Kerala, Vol. I, New Delhi, 1982 edition, p. 459.
4. Ibid., p. 460.
5. Cf. F.M. Hussnain, Buddhist Kashmir, 1973, p. 395.
6. Ibid., pp. 404-5.
7. H. Dhammaratana Thera, Buddhism in South India, Kandy, Sri Lanka, 1964, p. 18.
8. A. Sreedhara Menon, Cultural Heritage of Kerala - An Introduction, Cochin, 1978, p. 12.
9. K. Raghvan, Buddhist Relics in Kerala, The Maha Bodhi Calcutta, May 1972, p. 142.
10. Ibid., pp. 141, p. 142.
11. Ibid., p. 143.
12. T.A. Gopinatha Rao, Elements of Hindu Iconography, Vol. III, p. 487.
13. K.R. Vaidyanathan, Temples and Legends of Kerala, Bombay, 1982, p. 71.
14. T.A. Gopinatha Rao; Elements of Hindu Iconography, Vol. II, p. 486.
15. A. Sreedhara Menon, Cultural Heritage of Kerala, p. 27-28.
16. Ibid., pp. 27-28.

17. K.R. Vaidyanathan, Temples and Legends of Kerala, Bombay, 1982, p.4.

18. Srredhara Menon, Cultural Heritage of Kerala, p.72.

19. H.A. Giles, Record of the Buddhistiic Kingdoms (of Fa-Hsien) Varanasi, 1972, p.64.

20. D.C. Ahir, India's Debt to Buddhism, New Delhi,l 1964, p.86.

21. V.R. Parameswaran Pillai, Temple Culture of South India, New Delhi, 1986 pages 39-40.

22. Ibid., p.42.

23. Ibid.

7

Pondicherry

The de-facto merger with the Indian Union of Pondicherry, the former French colony, took place on Ist November 1954. Through a Constitutional Amendment on 28 December 1962, Pondicherry, Karaikal, Mahe and Yanam were constituted into an Union Territory of Pondicherry. In area, this Union Territory is 492 sq. km. comprising of Pondicherry (292 sq. km.) , Karaikal (160) sq. km.) Mahe (9 sq. km.) and Yanam (30 sq. km.). Pondicherry is bounded by the Bay of Bengal on the east and by South Arcot district of Tamil Nadu on the other sides.

In ancient days, Pondicherry was part and parcel of the Tondaimandalam Kingdom, the area around Kanchipuram. As in other parts of Tamil Nadu, Buddhism appears to have firmly reached Pondicherry in the third century BC during the reign of Asoka, the first Buddhist Emperor. There is evidence to show that during the Sangam Age (3rd century BC - 3rd century AD), there were Buddhist monks and monasteries in Pondicherry. At one time Arikkamedu, at the estaury of the river Ariyankuppam, near Pondicherry, was a flourishing commercial centre. It appears to have been destroyed some time after the Sangam Age. The scholars differ as to the exact meaning of the word Arikkamedu. The ruins of the ancient city are called by some scholars *Arukkumedu*, 'mound of ruins' or 'mound on a river bank' while others call it *Arukanmedu* meaning 'mound of Jina or

Buddha'.[1] The discovery of a Buddha statue[2] from the ruins of Arikkamedu is significant in this context. The lost city may have been once the stronghold of Buddhism. Hence, the 'mound of Buddha' may be its more appropriate name.

The total population of Pondicherry in 1981 was 604, 471. Out of it, the Buddhist population in Pondicherry was only 75. This indicates some improvement over the 1971 figure of 21.

Notes and References

1. A. Ramasamy, History of Pondicherry, New Delhi, 1987, p. 15.

2. Ibid., p. 19.

8

Tamil Nadu

The present day Tamil Nadu, the land of the Tamils, was formed in November 1956 consequent upon the reorganisation of the Indian States on linguistic basis in the light of the recommendations of the States Reorganisation Commission. Its capital is Madras, and in area Tamil Nadu is 1,30,069 sq. kms.

(I) ROYAL PATRONAGE

The first royal patron of Buddhism in the Tamil land was no doubt Asoka the Great. He built stupas at Kanchi in the third century BC. According to the Tamil classic, *Manimekhalai*, king Killivalan built a Buddha *Vihara* at Kanchi, The king is also said to have dedicated a park to the Buddhist *Sangha* in which a shrine containing an imprint of the Buddha's feet was also created. The first Pallava king, Skandavarman, who flourished towards the close of the third century AD, also helped the cause of Buddhism. He had a son, Buddhavarman, who is mentioned as Yuvaraj in a grant[1] issued by his queen, Charudevi, perhaps a Buddhist. His other son was Buddhyankara.

The history of Tamil Nadu, after Skandavarman till the sixth century is rather obscure. In the Tamil literature, this period is called as one of the darkest period of history, and the modern scholars often refer to this period as 'the Kalabhra Interregnum'. Not only that, the Kalabhras, who seem to have come to power in the Kanchipuram area, the Tondaimandalam, as it was then called, are called 'barbarians' and 'enemies' of civilization'. About this period, K.A. Nilakanta Sastri says[2]:

"A long historical night ensues after the close of the Sangam age. We know little of the period of more than three centuries that followed. When the curtain rises again towards the close of the sixth century A.D., we find a mysterious and ubiquitous enemy of civilization, the evil rulers called Kalabhras (Kalappalar), have come and upset the established political order which was restored only by their defeat at the hands of the Pandyas and Pallavas as well as the Chalukyas of Badami."

The identification of the Kalabhras is a big question mark on the South Indian History. It is now generally agreed that the Kalabhras originally hailed from the area around the modern Tirupati in Andhra, and had migrated to Kanchi sometime in the third century AD. The Tirupati hills were also known earlier as Pullikunram or the hill of the Chieftain Pulli. The Sangam Age literature refers to Pulli, the chief of the Kalavar tribes in the Venkata or Vengadam hills. "The name of the hill was Vengadam. Mamulanur, the most important and perhaps the oldest poet, has seven poems referring to Vengadam. He refers to Vengadam as belonging to Pulli, the Chieftain of Kalavar, and notes that Vengadam was famous for its festivals. In another poem he refers undoubtedly to Tirupati as Pullikunran, the Hill of Chieftain Pulli. Another poem says these Pullis were liberal in gifts.[3]:

The Pullis have been identified with the Kalavaras or the Kalabhras, who appeared to have migrated under political compulsions from their native place to Kanchi where they made fortune having established their rule there. According to Dr. S. Krishnaswami Aiyangar[4], "The tightening of the hold of the Pallavas even as viceroys of the Andhras by a pressure applied both from the north and west must have dislodged these people from the locality of their denzienship, and set forward their migration which ultimately overturned the Tondaimandalam first, Cholamandalam next and a considerable part of the

Pandimandalam after that .... the Kalabhras then were the Kalavar of the region immediately north of Tondaimandala who being dislodged by the pressure of the Andhras penetrated the Tondaimandalam itself, moved southwards till .... they produced the interregnum referred to in the Velvikkudi plates in the Pandya country.:"

About the identification of the Kalabhras, R. Sathianata Aiyer says[5]" "The identification of the Kalabhras is very difficult problem of South Indian History. They have been identified with the line of Muttaraivar of Kondubalur (eighth to eleventh century). Others regards them as Karnatas on the strength of a reference in Tamil literature to the rule of a Karnata king over Madura. A third view is that the Kalabhras were Kalappalar, belonging to Vellala community and referred to in Tamil literature and inscriptions. But the most satisfactory theory identifies the Kalabhras with the Kalavar, and the chieftains of this tribe mentioned in Sangam literature are Tiraiyan of Pavattiri and Pulli of Vengadam or Tirupati. The latter is described as the cattle lifting robber chief of the frontier. The Kalavar must have been dislodged from their habitat near Tirupati by political events of the third century A.D., viz. the fall of the Satvahanas, resulting in political confusion in Tondamandalam in the following century. The Kalabhra invasion must have overwhelmed the Pallavas, the Cholas and the Pandyas."

In the Brahmanical literature, the Kalabhras are "roundly denounced as evil kings (*kali-arasar*) who uprooted many adhirajas and abrogated *brahmadeya* rights". However, the modern researches have shown that the Kalabhras were neither barbarians nor enemies of civilization but were a very civilized people, and in fact their reign saw the creation of excellent Tamil literature. The primary reason as to why they were ignored or abused by the brahmins was because they were Buddhists. To quote Nilakanta Sastri again[6]: "...... from some Buddhist books we hear of a certain Acchutavikkanta of the Kalabhrakula during whose reign Buddhist monasteries and authors enjoyed much patronage in the Chola country. Late literary tradition in Tamil avers that he kept in confinement the three Tamil kings - the Chera, Chola and Pandya. Some songs about him are quoted by Amitasagara, a Jain grammarian of Tamil of the tenth century A.D. Possibly Accuta was himself a Buddhist, a political revolution which the Kalabhras effected was provoked by religious antagonism."

The only Kalabhra king who is known with a specific name is Accuta Vikranta. He is believed to have ruled towards the close of the fifth century AD and the beginning of the sixth century AD. Buddhadatta, a well-known Pali commentator who flourished in the fifth century says in the *Vinaya-viniccaya* that "he wrote this work for the sake of Buddhasiha while he was residing in the lovely monastery of Venhudas (Vishnudas) in a city on the banks of the Kaveri, by name Bhutamangalam and it was begun and completed at the time when Accuta Vikranta of Kalabhra Kula was ruling over the earth[7].:

The memory of Accuta Vikranta lingered on for long among the Tamil Buddhists. In *Yapparungalam,* a Tamil work of eleventh century AD, written by Amitasagarangar, the poet "prays to the Buddha to grant Accuta with the long arms like the clouds in charity and with the fighting spear so that he might wield his specture of authority over the whole world".[8] From the testimony of Buddhadatta, who was contemporary of Accuta Vikranta, and the praise showered upon the Kalabhra king by the poet in *Yapparungalam,* it is evident that Acchuta Vikranta was a Buddhist and a liberal patron of Buddhism.

It is significant that during the Kalabhra reign which lasted nearly 300 years, Buddhism was at its best in and around Kanchi, ancient Tondaimandalam. And there flourished a number of Buddhist saints and scholars, such as Nagaguttanar, author of *Kundalakesi,* (4th century), Buddhadatta, the Pali commentator, (5th century), Dinnaga, the great logician, (5th century), Dhammapala, another Pali commentator, (6th century), and Bodhidharma, the great Dhyana teacher, (6th century). The association of Buddhaghosha, the greatest Pali scholar and commentator, who was contempoary of Buddhadatta, further confirms the ascendency of Buddhism during the Kalabhra Interregnum in the Tamil land.

Even the Tamil literature got a boost during the Kalabhra reign and this period was marked by great literary activity. Nilakanta Sastri observes [9]: "This dark period marked by the ascendency of Buddhism and probably also of Jainism, was characterized also by great literary activity in Tamil. Most of the works grouped under the head The Eighteen Minor Works were written during this period as also the *Silappadikaram, Manimekhalai* and other works. Many of the authors were the votaries of the 'heretical' sects.

The Kalabhras were ousted by the Pallavas who rose to prominence again under Simhavishnu (575-600 AD) who founded a new dynasty which ruled for nearly 300 years. During the reign of the Pallava king, Narasimhavarman II (c. 700-728 or 695-722), a Buddhist *Vihara*[10] was constructed at Nagapattam for the use of the Chinese mariners who called over there for purposes of trade. This monastery was known as the Chinese monastery and was seen by Marco Polo in 1292 AD.

During the reign of the Cholas (850-1200 AD), there were Buddhist settlements at Nagapattam (Nagapattinam) on the east coast and at Srimulvasam in the west. Raja Raja I, (985-1014 AD), in particular, gave generous support to the Buddhist institutions[11]. And even Buddhism was, considered sufficiently important for some scenes from Buddha's life to be represented in decorative panels in a balustrade of the great temple at Tanjore (Thanjavur) built by him. He also encouraged Sri Mara Vijayayottunagavarman, the Sailendra ruler of Sri Vijaya (Sumatra) to build a Buddha *Vihara* at Nagapatam. This *Vihara* was called *Sri Cudamani Vihara*[12] after the father of the ruler of Sri Vijaya. Later, another Sri Vijaya king sent embassy in 1090 to the Chola King Kolottunga I (1070-1122) to enquire[13] about the affairs of the Buddha *Vihara* which his ancestors had built at Nagapattam. Chola endowments[14] to the Buddha *Vihara* at Nagapattam have also been recorded in their copper-plate grants.

Evidence of royal support to Buddhism after the Chola period is lacking, though the Buddha Viharas at Nagapattam flourished till about the 17th century.

(II) BUDDHIST SAINTS AND SCHOLARS

1. Ilambodhiyar

The first Tamil Buddhist poet was Ilambodhiyar who flourished during the last Sangam period of Tamil literature (1st-2nd century AD). Ilambodhiyar's very name indicates that he was a Buddhist. Since the Buddhists worshipped the Bodhi Tree, the Shaiva and Jaina Tamil works often refer to Buddhists as "bodhiyar"[15] or worshippers of Bodhi tree. Several verses of Ilambodhiyar are found in a work called *Nattrinai* or *Narrinai* composed during the last Sangam period.

2. Sittalai Sattanar

The most famous Buddhist poet in the Tamil land was Sittalai Sattanar, the author of the celebrated Tamil epic *Manimekhalai*. Sattanar was a grain merchant of Madura (Madurai) and lived in the second century AD. The *Manimekhalai* appears to have been composed by him with a view to propagating the Buddha-Dhamma but its setting is historical. Another great Tamil epic, the *Silappadikaram* (The Book of the Anklet), written by Ilango-Adigal, a Jaina ascetic and brother of the Chera monarch, Senguttuvan, deals with the tragic story of Kovalan, a rich merchant of Kaveripattinam or Puhar who neglecting his wife, Kannaki, fell in love with Madhavi, a dancing girl. Later, having realized his folly, Kovalan returned to his wife. Then both set out for Madura where Kovalan wanted to start life afresh by pursuing trade. And when he went out to sell one of his wife's gold anklet, he was falsely accused of theft of queen's anklet, and was executed by the king without any investigation.

On hearing the news of the death of Kovalan, Madhavi became disgusted with life. She, alongwith her daughter, Manimekhalai, sought solace from a Buddhist monk, who consoled in her grief preaching the true *Dhamma*. The young Manimekhalai was so much impressed by the teaching of love and compassion of the Buddha that she became a Buddhist nun, Bhikkhuni. While narrating the story of Manimekhalai, Sattanar shows the superiority of Buddhist doctrine evaluating it against the contemporary Hindu and Jaina thought. *Manimekhalai* "is a lasting monument to his scholarship, encylopaedic knowledge, and excellence as a Tamil poet[16]."

Several verses from other poems of Sittalai Sattanar are found in other works[17], such as, *Nattrinai, Kurunthokai, Purananuru* and *Ahananuru*.

3. Aravana Adigal

Aravana Adigal was the first Tamilian Buddhist monk who engaged himself in propagating the *Dhamma* in the ancient Chera, Chola and Pandyan kingdoms of South India. He lived in the second century AD, and was the head of a flourishing Buddhist monastery[18] at Kaveripattinam, also known as Puhar. This illustrious monk was the preceptor of Manimekhalai, whose life story has been told by Sittlai Sattanar, in the classic Tamil epic, entitled *'Manimekhalai'*. When Kaveripattinam was ravaged by a tidal wave, Aravana Adigal went to Vanchi or Vanji, the Chera capital, where he stayed for a short while before moving on to Kanchi. Manimekhalai, who had earlier embraced Buddhism and joined the Sangha, the Order of the Buddhist nuns, also followed in the footsteps of his preceptor, and came to live at Kanchi. What was the righteous path of the Dhamma expounded by Aravana Adigal has been summed up by the poet in Book XXX of *Manimekhalai*. The saint begins with the Four Noble Truths and then goes on to explain the essence of twelve Nidanas, (Dependent Origination) and finally exhorts Manimekhalai in these words[19]:

"Realizing that friendliness, compassion and joy (at the well-being of others) constitute the best attitude of mind, give up anger. By the practice of hearing (*sruti*), mentation (*cintana*), experiencing in mind (*bhavana*) and realizing in vision (*darsana*), reflect, realize give up all illusion. In these four ways get rid of the darkness of mind."

4. Manimekhalai

The daughter of Madhavi from Kovalan, Manimekhalai, is the heroine of the famous Tamil epic, named after her, and written by Sittali Sattanar. When Kovalan was executed on a false accusation by the king of Madura (Madurai), Madhavi became disgusted with the life, and sought solace in her-grief from Aravana Adigal, a Buddhist monk, who was head of a Buddhist monastery at Keveripattinam (Puhar). On hearing the excellent Dhamma, both mother and daughter became Buddhists. The young and pretty Manimekhalai, who was already feeling disenchanted by the life of dance and music, was immediately drawn to the sublime teachings of the Buddha and decided to adopt the life of a Buddhist nun. Soon thereafter, she went on pilgrimage to Sri Lanka and worshipped at the Buddha's footprint at the Nagadipa shrine on an island off the northern coast of Sri Lanka. There a deity gave her a miraculous bowl from which she could feed any number of people without the supply of food becoming exhausted. On return to Kaveripattinam, Manimekalai gave alms daily to the poor in a public hall. Later, Manimekhalai was implicated in a murder case on a false charge and imprisoned. When, however, true facts came to light, she was freed, and the Chola queen, who had manipulated her imprisonment, begged her pardon.

Realizing that it was no longer safe for her to live in Kaveripattinam, Manimekhalai went on a pilgrimage to Java. On return from this pilgrimage, she went to Vanchi, the Chera capital, and further studied the *Dhamma*. Finally, she came to Kanchi where in the meanwhile Aravana Adigal, her preceptor, had permanently settled. Thereafter, she lived the holy life of a Buddhist nun in a Vihara specifically built for her at Kanchi, and spent her life in meditation and service to humanity. The present day *Darupadiamman kovil* is said to be on the site of the *Manimekhalai Vihara*.

5. Nagaguttanar

Nagaguttanar[20], who lived in the fourth century AD, was another Buddhist poet of eminence. He was the author of *Kundalakesi,* one of the five famous kavyas in Tamil language. The story of Kundalakesi in this work is based on the biography of the bhikkhuni Kundalakesi found in the commentary on the Therigatha as well as in the Dhammapada commentary. While narrating the story, the author had made an effort to refute the Vedic and Jaina dectrines. Kundalakesi was originally a Jain nun, who was fond of challenging anybody to refute her views. Sariputta, the chief disciple of the Buddha, took up the challenge and defeated her in a debate. Consequently, Kundalakesi renounced Jainism and embraced Buddhism. The author of the Tamil poem depicts the Buddhist nun Kundalakesi championing the cause of Buddhism. *Kundalakesi* is now lost, But the Jaina work *Nilakesi,* written in response to *Kundalakesi,* is still extant, and the Jain work contains references to *Kundalakesi.* A commentary on the *Nilakesi* also refers to the story of Kundalakesi.

6. Buddhadatta

The first Pali scholar of Tamil Nadu was Buddhadatta. He was born at Uragapura, modern Uraiyur[21], in the fifth century AD. He studied Pali and Buddhism at the Mahavihara at Anuradhapura in Sri Lanka. Buddhadatta was contemporary of the great Pali scholar and commentator, Buddhaghosha. It is said that when Buddhadatta was returning to India after completing his studies, his boat crossed another boat carrying Buddhaghosha to Sri Lanka. As they met, they introduced themselves and exchanged pleasantries. On knowing Buddhaghosha's plans, Buddhadatta while departing requested Buddhaghosha to send copies of the commentaries, as and when compiled, to him in India. Buddhaghosha appears to have done this.

On return from Sri Lanka, Buddhadatta resided in a Vihara, built by a Buddhist minister named Krishnadasa, at Kaveripattanam. While staying here, he wrote *Madhurattha*

Vilasini (Commentary on the Buddhavamsa). He wrote another famous work *Abhidhammavatara* (Summary of Buddhaghosha's commentaries on the Abhidhammapitaka) at the request of a bhikkhu named Sumati. His another important work is *Vinaya Vinicchaya* (Summary of the Buddhaghosha's commentaries on the Vinaya-Pitaka). In a colophone at the end of this work, Buddhadatta says that "he wrote this work for the sake of Buddhasiha while he was residing in the lovely monastery of Vehnudasa (Vishnudasa) in a city on the banks of the river Kaveri, by name Bhutamangalam, and it was begun and completed at the time when Accuta Vikranta of Kalabhra Kula was ruling over the earth[22]".

Another work attributed to Buddhadatta is the *Uttara Vinicchya* which he is said to have written while he was residing at Anuradhapura.

7. Buddhaghosha

The greatest Pali scholar and commentator was Buddhaghosha who flourished in the fifth century AD. According to Mahavamsa[23], a chronicle of Sri Lanka, where Buddhaghosha accomplished his literary pursuits, he was born in the vicinity of Bodh Gaya. Another tradition is that he hailed from South India. K.R. Srinivasan contends that Buddhaghosha was born at Morandakhetaka which he identifies with Moranam[24] near Kanchi.

By the time Buddhaghosha came on the scene Pali Buddhism had lost lustre in India. More and more scholars were turning to Sanskrit. But the Bodh Gaya monks stood firm in their allegiance to Pali. Under their guidance, Buddhaghosha studied Buddhist philosophy diligently. He also compiled a treatise on Buddhism *'Nanodaya'*. He also planned to compose commentaries on Abhidhamma and the Suttas. On knowing his intention, his teacher, Maha Thera Revata advised Buddhaghosha to go to Sri Lanka.

Thus encouraged and inspired, Buddhaghosha went to Sri Lanka during the reign of King Mahanama (410-432) AD and reached the Mahavihara at Anuradhapura. While staying in the Mahavihara, Buddhaghosha made a thorough study of the Sinhalese commentaries. He also heard the tradition of the elders from Thera Sanghapala. Convinced of their usefulness, he then sought permission of the bhikkhu-Sangha of the Mahavihara to translate the commentaries from Sinhalese to Pali. In order to test his knowledge and his capabilities, the learned Theras asked Buddhaghosha to comment on a Pali stanza. In response to this, Buddhaghosha compiled a compendium of the whole of the Tripitaka, and named it *Visuddhimagga* or "The Path of Purification." Highly pleased with his performance, the bhikkhus of the Mahavihara gave all the facilities to Buddhaghosha and placed all the Sinhalese commentaries at the disposal.

Besides the *Visuddhimagga,* Buddhaghosha wrote commentaries on the *Vinaya-Pitaka, Patimokha, Digha-Nikaya, Majjhima-Nikaya, Anguttara-Nikaya, Khuddaka-Patha.* The commentaries on the *Dhammapada* and the *Jataka* are also ascribed to Buddhaghosha. The voluminous literature produced by Buddhaghosha exists to this day and "is the basis for the explanation of many crucial points of Buddhist philosophy which without them would have been unintelligible." The commentaries and the *Visuddhimagga* of Buddhaghosha are not only a great achievement in post-Tripitaka literature but they are also a key to the Tripitaka.

Buddhaghosha may or may not have been born in Tamil Nadu but the fact remains that he resided for some time at Kanchi and compiled some of the commentaries while staying there. In the colopohon to the commentary on the Anguttara Nikaya, *Manorathapurani,* Buddhaghosha says[25] that at the time of compiling the work he lived at Kanchipura with his friend Bhikkhu Jotipala. Again in the commentary on the Majjhima Nikaya, *Papancasudani,* he says[26] that 'when he was formerly living at Mayrrapattanam (the present day Mayavaram), with the Thera Buddhamitta, he was invited to write this'. Buddhaghosha had also visited Nagapattanam, the port city, from where he had embarked for Sri Lanka.

8. Dhammapala

Another Pali scholar produced by Tamil Nadu was Dhammapala. He lived in the sixth century AD, and was a native of the city of Tanja, which has been identified with Tanjore (Tanjavur). According to Hiuen Tsang, Dhammapala was born at Kanchipuram. Dhammapala also stayed for some time at Nagapattam in the Dharmasoka *Vihara.* In the *Nettipakarna* commentary, Dhammapala says[27] that "he wrote this commentary while he was residing at the monastery built by King Asoka at Nagapattam which is like unto a port for embarking on the ocean of the Dhamma".

Most probably, Dhammapala had studied at Anuradhapura in Sri Lanka as he mentions in his works the *Atthakathas* of the Mahavihara of Anuradhapura. Further, he not only refers to the commentaries of Buddhaghosha but also follows almost his style. Dhammapala wrote seven commentaries on such books of the *Khuddaka-Nikaya,* which had not been covered by Buddhaghosha. His famous work the *Parmattha-dipani,* is an exposition of the *Khuddaka-Nikaya* covering mainly *Udana, Itivuttka, Vimanavatthu, Peta-Vatthu, Thera-gatha, Theri-gatha,* and *Cariya-Pitaka.* The other commentaries attributed to Dhammapala are : *Parmattha-manjusas* (Commentary on Buddhaghosha's Visuddhimagga), and *Netti-Pakarnassa Attha Samvannana* (Commentary on Netti, a post-canonical work).

9. Dinnaga

A mighty Buddhist intellectual of the early fifth century AD was Dinnaga or Dignaga. He was the founder of the Buddhist logic, and is often referred to as the Father of the medieval *Nyaya* as a whole.

Dinnaga was born around 450 AD at Simhavaktra,[28] a suburb of Kanchipuram in Tamil Nadu. After completing his studies, while quite young, Dinnaga became a Buddhist monk and joined the Vatsiputriya school. It is said that one day, Nagadatta, his preceptor, asked Dinnaga "to meditate over the principle of the

Ego (*Atman*) which from the stand point of the Vatsiputriyas was inexpressible and was neither identical with the groups of elements (*Skandhas*), nor differing from them." When Dinnaga expressed some scepticism about the existence of Ego, he was expelled from the community by his teacher. After meeting similar failure and experiencing dissatisfaction with some other teachers, Dinnaga finally came to Vasubandhu. Under Vasubandhu, Dinnaga studied all aspects of the Buddhist philosophy and became well-versed with all the texts of Buddhism. Thereafter, he began his literary career.

Dinnaga travelled all over India holding religious contests with scholars. At Nalanda, he defeated a Brahmin logician named Sadurjaya in a religious discussion. In Orissa, Dinnaga is said to have converted the royal treasurer, Bhadrapalita, who built in Dinnaga's honour a monastery. Generally, Dinnaga stayed in this monastery in the Bhorasila mountain in Orissa. Often he also stayed in the Accra monastery in Maharashtra.

Dinnaga wrote about a hundred treatises on logic, most of which are preserved in Chinese and Tibetan translations. His most important works are: *Pramanasamuccaya* (The Totality of Means of Correct Knowledge). *Alambana-Pariksha* (The Examination of the Three Times), *Hetuchakradamru* (The Wheel of Logical Reasons), *Nyaya-mukha, Hastavala-prakarna, Arya Prajnaparmitavivarana,* and *Abhidharmakosha-Marma-Pradipa,* a commentary on Vasubandhu's Abhidharmakosa.

Prior to Dinnaga, all the Indian schools of logic followed the logic of the realist Nyaya school. Dinnaga for the first time introduced new ideas in that logic, which then came to be recognised as Buddhist logic.

10. Bodhidharma

An outstanding Indian missionary who went to China was Bodhidharma, a seer of royal family of Kanchi in Tamil Nadu. On joining the Buddhist Sangha, he was initiated into Buddhism by Prajnatara, a renowned teacher of the *Dhyana* or meditative form of Buddhism. After his teacher's death, he worked for few years to popularise the Dhyana teachings in India. Later, he left for China in A.D. 526 for propagating his system of philosophy.

Bodhidharma was cordially welcomed by the emperor Wu-ti, who was a devout Buddhist, at his capital, Nanking. Later, finding that the emperor was not able to appreciate his mystic trend of philosophy, Bodhidharma left the capital, and went to the Shaolin monastery, near Lo-yang, in north China.

It is said that Bodhidharma sat at the Shao-lin Temple doing *pi-kuan,* deeply absorbed in contemplation with his face to the wall, without interacting with others for nine years[29] In Chinese, *pi* means "wall" and *kuan* means "observation". Thus Bodhidharma is well-known for *pi-kuan* or "wall meditation" in China. He lays stress on meditation by which alone, he said, "enlightenment should be attained". The meditative school founded by Bodhidharma is known as *Ch'an* Buddhism in China. The *Ch' an* or *Dhyana* School teaches that we must discard blind acceptance of scriptural authority. It also deprecates the worship of images and priestcraft. According to it, "Buddha is in the heart of man. And Buddha-nature is always pure and bright, illuminating everywhere." The mystic philosophy of Bodhidharma has exercised an abiding spiritual influence among the Japanese Buddhists, where the *Ch'an* Buddhism became *Zen* Buddhism[30] (contemplative Buddhism) with certain modifications.

11. Dharmapala

Dharmapala was the only South Indian Buddhist savant who became the Vice-Chancellor of the world famous Nalanda University, He was born at Kanchi in the seventh century AD. It is said that when he was about to be married, he secretly went to a Buddhist monastery and joined the Buddhist *Sangha.* Hiuen Tsang gives the traditional account of Dharmapala's initiation into Buddhism as under[31] : "The city of Kanchipura is the native place of Dharmapala Bodhisattva. He was the eldest son of a great minister of the country. From his childhood he exhibited much cleverness, and as he grew up it increased and extended.

When he became a young man, the king and queen condescended to entertain him at a (marriage) feast. On the evening of the day his heart was oppressed with sorrow, and being exceedingly afflicted, he placed himself before a statue of Buddha and engaged in earnest prayer (supplication). Moved by his extreme sincerity, the spirits removed him to a distance, and there he hid himself. After going many hundred li from this spot he came to a mountain convent, and sat down in the hall of Buddha. A priest happening to open the door, and seeing this youth, was in doubt whether he was a robber or not. After interrogating him on the point, the Bodhisattva completely unbosomed himself and told him the cause; moreover he asked permission to become a disciple. The priests were much astonished at the wonderful event, and forthwith granted his request. The king ordered search to be made for him in every direction and at length finding out that Bodhisattva had removed to a distance from the world, driven by the spirit (or, spirits), then he redoubled his deep reverence and admiration for him. From the time that Dharmapala assumed the robes of a recluse, he applied himself with unflagging earnestness to learning. Concerning his brilliant reputation we have spoken in the previous records."

Dharmapala travelled widely in India. While at Kosambi, he in a debate with the opponents of Buddhism displayed his brilliant oratory and encylopaedic knowledge tearing to shreds the arguments of the Hindu scholars. He became famous after this victory, and was selected to head the Nalanda Mahavihara. He died quite young at the age of 32. His pupil Silabhadra, succeeded him as Vice-Chancellor, under whom Hiuen Tsang studied Buddhism at Nalanda.

12. Dharmakirti

Dharmakirti, who lived in the seventh century AD, was another great Buddhist logician. He was the son of Korunanda of Tirumalaya[32] in South India. In his childhood, Dharmakirti studied the Vedas. Later, he studied Buddhist philosophy at Nalanda. While at Nalanda, Dharmakirti joined the Buddhist

Order as a disciple of Dharmapala who was at that time the Sanghasthavira (Chief) of the Nalanda Mahavihara. He studied logic from Isvarsena, a direct pupil of Dinnaga, and made a thorough study of the *Pramanasamuccaya* of Dinnaga. The date of Dharmakirti is not very clear. Some scholars are of the view that he lived from circa AD 620-690.[33]

Dharmakirti wrote seven important works. These are 1. *Pramanavartika*, 2. *Pramanavinischaya*, 3. *Nyayabindu*, 4. *Hetubindu*, 5. *Vadanyaya*, 6. *Sambandhaparikasha*, and 7. *Santanantarasidhi*. As in other cases, all the works of Dharmakirti were lost in India. For a long time in modern India, nothing was known of Dharmakirti's works except *Nyayabindu*. Thanks are due to the Tibetan scholars who preserved his works, some in original Sanskrit and all in Tibetan translation. In modern times, credit goes to Mahapandit Rahul Sankrityayan who made many hazardous trips to Tibet and brought back to India some of the manuscripts of Dharmakirti's works in Sanskrit and commentaries on them. Rahul Sankrityayana also edited Dharmakirti's monumental work *Pramanavartika* with three commentaries, as well as *Vadanyaya*.

All the works of Dharmakirti generally deal with the Buddhist theory of knowledge. Dharmakirti was a subtle philosophical thinker and dialectician, and his writings mark the highest summit reached in epistemological speculation by later Buddhism. Acknowledging his unsurpassed genious, Dr. Stcherbatksy calls Dharmakirti, the Kant of India.

Apart from being a great Buddhist logician and philosopher, Dharmakirti was also a great missionary. He travelled throughout India and tried to re-establish, through philosophy, the glory of Buddhism which was showing signs of decline.

13. Bodhiruchi

Bodhiruchi, which literally means "intelligence loving", was originally called Dharmaruchi. He hailed from Tamil Nadu and wen to China in the seventh century AD during the days of early

T' ang dynasty. His original name Dharmaruchi was changed[34] to Bodhiruchi by the orders of the empress Wu Tso-thien (AD 684-705). In China, he studied Buddhism under Yasaghosa, a Mahayana Thera and became well-acquainted with the entire Tripitaka within a period of only three years. Thereafter, Bodhiruchi devoted all his time and talents to the work of translating Sanskrit works. During the period AD 693-713, he translated 53 works which ran into 111 volumes in Chinese. He is said to have died in AD 727 when he was in his 156th year.

14. Vajrabodhi

Vajrabodhi (661-730) was born at Podiyakanda in the Pandya country[35]. Another view is that he was a native of Kanchi. He studied at Nalanda, and returned to his native place as a Mahayana monk. He was contemporary of the Pallava king, Narasimhavarman II (c.700-728 AD). His missionary tours took him to Sri Lanka where he stayed for six months at the Abhayagiri Vihara. Later, along with his disciple Amoghavajra, he went to China for missionary work. He is said to have carried the text of *Mahaprajnaparamita* with him to China. Vajrabodhi also translated a number of Buddhist works into Chinese. He passed away in China in the year 730 AD.

15. Bodhisena

Bodhisena, a venerable monk of Madurai[36] In Tamil Nadu, was the first Indian Buddhist monk to go to Japan and propagate the Buddha-Dhamma there. It is said that a Japanese monk, Tazi-hi-marito had come to India in about 723 AD to learn more about Buddhism., He met Bodhisena, who was a renowned orator, writer and scholar of Buddhism at that time, and they became good friends. Later, Bodhisena was invited by Emperor Shomu to Japan. Accordingly, he sailed for Japan via South Sea and reached Japan in 736 AD. Impressed by his knowledge of the teachings of the Buddha, in particular, his understanding of the *Buddha-avatamsaka-Mahavaipulya-sutra,* Emperor Shomu invited Ven. Bodhisena to perform the consecration ceremony of the

Maha-Vairochana Buddha. Thus Bodhisena had the honour to act as the officiating Minister at the historic ceremony in 749 AD of the Great Buddha at Nara. Bodhisena passed away in Japan at the age of 57 in 760 AD.

16. Buddhamitra

Buddhamitra was born at Ponparri village of Arantangi taluk of Tanjore district.[37] He was a reputed Tamil teacher and preacher. Buddhamitra was contemporary of the Chola king, Virarajendra, who ruled from 1063-1070. On the request of the Chola King, Buddhamitra wrote a comprehensive Tamil grammer, and named it 'Virasoliyam', after his royal patron. Buddhamitra, who was a Mahayana Bhikkhu, not only refers to the Buddha-Dhamma in the concluding varses of the Tamil grammer but also invariably mentions the Buddha and His virtues while giving examples for the purpose of elucidating rhetorical devices.

17. Anuruddha

Anuruddha Thera, who flourished in the early part of the twelfth century, was a reputed scholar of Pali and Buddhism. He was born at Kaveripattnam[38] but he spent best part of his life at Kanchi. He was associated with the Mulasomavihara of Kanchi which he headed for sometime. During his missionary preachings, Anuruddha Thera also visited other Buddhist centres like Tirunelveli and Tanjavur. He also visited Sri Lanka where he did missionary work during the reign of Vijayabahu II (1065-1120 AD). Anuruddha Thera was a reputed scholar of Pali and Buddhism. His most famous work *'Asbhidhammattha-Sangaha'* the Manual of Psychology and Ethics, has served as an introduction to the *Abhidhamma* philosophy ever since it was written, and is still popular in Burma and Sri Lanka. Two other works attributed to Anuruddha Thera are: *Pamattha-vinicchaya* and *Namarupa-pariccheda*; the latter being a philosophical poem, but his authorship of these two is doubted by some scholars.

18. Dispankara Buddhapiya Thera

Dipankara Buddhapiya Thera was another Pali scholar of repute. He lived in the twelfth century. He went to Sri lanka where he studied Pali and Buddhism under the venerable Ananda Vanaratana. While in Sri Lanka, he wrote the Pali grammer *'Rupasiddhi'* which is even today used in the monastic colleges. In the concluding part of the *Rupasiddhi,* he says that he was born in the Chola country[39] and resided for sometime in Sri Lanka. His other book *Pajjamadhu'* (Nector of Verses) contains beautiful Pali varses in praise of the Buddha. On return from Sri Lanka, he became the abbot of the Baladitya monastery in the Chola country.

19. Kassapa Thera

Another Cholian[40] Buddhist monk who lived in the twelfth century and spent some time in Sri Lanka and was a great scholar of Pali and Buddhism was Kassapa Thera. he too studied in Sri Lanka. His works include a commentary on the Abhidhamma, called *'Moha Vicchedani,* and a commentary on the Vinaya Pitaka, called *Vimati Vinodani'* and the *"Anagatavamsa"*. In the concluding part of the *'Mohavicchedani'* Kassapa Thera says that he was a resident of 'Nagana monastery' in Nagapattanam of the Chola country.

20. Dhammakitti Thera

Dhammakitti or Dharmakirti Thera was another Cholian[41] monk who went to Sri Lanka and engaged himself in the literary work. He wrote the first part of *Culavamsa,* which is a continuation of the famous chronicle of Sri Lanka, *Mahavamsa.* Beginning from King Sirimevan, he added events upto his own time. The *Dathavamsa,* a chronicle of the Tooth Relic, is also ascribed to him. Ven. Dharmakirti also organised an International Buddhist Conference in Sri Lanka under the patronage of Parakrama Bahu II.

(III) BUDDHIST SITES AND SHRINES

I. Kanchipuram

Kanchi, Kanchinpura or Kanchipuram (Conjeevaram), just 70 kilometres form Madras, was the epicentre of Buddhism in the ancient Tamil land. The first Buddhist edifices to be built at Kanchi were by Asoka the Great in the third century BC. He built stupas over all the sacred spots where the Buddha, according to tradition, had preached the *Dhamma*. In due course, many Buddhist shrines were built by the people of Kanchipuram.

In the Tamil classic of 2nd century AD, *Manimekhalai*, it is stated that King Killivalan built a Buddhist temple in the city, and that the king also dedicated a park named 'Tarumadavana' to the Buddhist *Sangha*. A shrine containing an imprint of the Buddha's feet is also said to have been erected in the park. Aravana Adigal, a renowned Buddhist saint at that time migrated to Kanchi from Kaveripattnam after the latter was submerged by tidal waves. Manimekhalai, who had become a Buddhist nun, after listening to the *Dhamma* discourse from Aravana Adigal, also lived in this city and had a *Vihara* named after her.

Arya Deva, the chief disciple of Nagarjuna, spent the last years of his life at Kanchi in the third century AD. He is said to have been assassinated by one of his inmical disciples in a monastery at Ranganatha, a suburb of Kanchipuram. The famous Pali author and commentator, Buddhaghosha, who flourished in the fifth century AD, also resided for some time at Kanchi. In the concluding part of the commentary on the Anguttara Nikaya, *Manorathapurani*, Buddhaghosha says that he compiled this work while staying with his friend Bhikkhu Jotipala at Kanchipura. Similarly, in the commentary on the Majjhima Nikaya, *Papancasudani*, he says that the book was written by him while staying with Bhikkhu Buddhamitta at Mayrapattnam (the present Mayavaram near Kanchipuram). Some other prominent Buddhist saints and scholars associated with Kanchipuram were : Buddhadatta (5th Century AD.), Dinnaga (6th century AD), Bodhidharma (6th Century AD), Vajrabodhi (7th century AD), and Dharmapala (7th century AD).

When Hiuen Tsang, the Chinese pilgrim, visited Kanchipura in AD 639, Buddhism was still flourshing in this historic city. He says[42]

"This (Dravida) country is about 6000 li in circuit; the capital of the country is called Kanchipura, and is about 30 li round.... There are some hundred of *sangharamas* and 10,000 priests. They all study the teaching of the Sthavira (*Chang-tso-pu*) school belonging to the Great Vehicle. There are some eighty Deva temples, and many heretics called Nigranthas. Tathagata in olden days, when living in the world, frequented this country much; he preached the law here and converted men, and therefore Asoka-raja built *stupas* over all the sacred spots where these traces exist."

That Buddhism was a living religion at Kanchipuram as late as the 14th century is confirmed by the following evidence:

(i) According to an inscription[43] dated 1378 AD discovered in Korea, an Indian monk called Dhyanabhadra was the son of a king of Magadha and a princess from Kanchi and that when he visited Kanchi he heard a sermon given by a Buddhist preacher on the *Karanda-vyuha-sutra*.

(ii) A Javanese poem,[44] the *Nagarketagama* (14th century AD) tells us that Buddhatiya, a monk of Sadvihara at Kanchi composed laudatory poems (*bhogavali*) in praise of his contemporary Javanese king, Hayam Wuruk.

(iii) The commander-in-chief of Bhuvanaikabahu IV of Sri Lanka (14th century) is said to have built a Buddha *Vihara*[45] at Kanchi.

When Buddhism declined in Tamil Nadu, most of the Buddhist temples were either converted into Hindu temples or pulled down and the material used in building the new Hindu temples. Because of this trend of conversion of Buddhist edifices into Hindu temples or demolishing them and building the new Hindu temples on the same premises, the archaeologists have not been able to uncover any significant Buddhist remains at Kanchi. The solitary discovery of the remains of a Buddhist stupa dated second or first century BC was made by a team of the Madras University in 1971 which carried excavations right in the middle of the temple town near the *Kamahshi Amman* temple. However, Kanchipuram has yielded a large number of Buddha images covering a period of nearly 800 years from sixth century to fourteenth century AD.

The "most remarkable" Buddha image dating to sixth or seventh century AD was discovered by T.A. Gopinatha Rao in 1915. He discovered this image in the innermost *prakara* of the *Kamakshi amman* temple at Kanchi. Mr. Rao says[46] : "The total height of the image is 7'10". Its two hands are broken; wherefore it is not possible to state definetly what they carried; presumably the right hand was held in the *abhaya* pose and the left carried an alms bowl. The nose is much worn; otherwise the image is in an excellent state of preservation. The long flowing robes descending from the left hand and the folds of the same over the right thigh are exquisitely worked." The discovery of this image from the innermost part of the present Hindu temple indicates that the *Kamakshi Amman* temple is a converted one. This remarkable Buddha image is now preserved in the Government Museum, Madras where it adorns the Buddhist sculpture gallery. According to P.R. Srinivasan, this figure is the earliest known example of Buddhist sculpture of Tamil land, as more ancient examples, have not been met with so far. He says:[47] "The importance of this figure is therefore manifold, namely, that it is a fine specimen of the art of sculpture of the early Pallava period; it is a landmark in the history of Buddhism in Tamil land and it presupposes the existence of a very important and probably a big Buddhist temple dating from about 600 A.D. in the heart of Kanchipuram".

Like the *Kamakshi Amman* temple, the *Karukkilamarndaamman* temple at Kanchi also appears to have been built on the site of a Buddha Vihara. Two remarkable Buddha images found in this Hindu temple have been described by Srinivasan as follows[48]:

"Seated Buddha, height about 3 feet 9 inches. It is found in the *Karukkilamarndaamman* temple at Kanchipuram and shows further development in its iconographic details. Here the Buddha is in the *bhusparsa mudra*. The features of the face and head, though pronounced, are in the classical style. The face here is of the Chola type. The noteworthy feature of this figure is the halo behind its head. It is beautifully worked with tassels inside and flame on the outside margin and with makara heads at both the lower ends which are shown touching the shoulders. The general treatment of the figure is evidently of a very high order and its date may therefore be about the beginning of the 12th century".

"Buddha, height 2 feet 6 inches, from *Karukkilamarnda amman* temple, Kanchipuram may be said to belong to a slightly subsequent period. The features are all pronounced, although the expression in the face and the general style of the figure go to show that it is still in the classical tradition. The most conspicuous of the features which suggests the late dating of the figure is the *prabhavali* behind its head. It is now supported on pilasters carved on either side of the figure, quite unlike the *prabhas* of the figures noticed above."

Yet another Hindu temple at Kanchipuram built on the site of a Buddha Vihara or with the material from a Buddhist temple is the *Ekamresvara* temple.[49] On the outer wall of this temple is a Buddha image in reclining posture (Mahaparinirvana posture). This figure is a unique specimen of its kind as no other Buddha image in the *Parinirvana* pose has been discovered in Tamil Nadu. The image has an oblong bhadra pitha. On the right end of this pitha and below the double-lotus design is a minature figure with hands in *anjali* pose held above the head and the face indicating extreme resourse. This figure may be of Ananda, the personal attendant of the Buddha. Other Buddha images of the *Ekamresvara* temple include one set carved in high relief in the dhyana pose *padmasana* within an elaborately worked prabha-on-pillar motif.

Another Buddha statue[50] discovered at Kanchipuram is near the Police Station at (Siva) Kanchi. It is datable to eleventh century. An interesting part of it is that its face is of the Javenese type rather than of the indigenous Chola type.

These are some of the significant Buddhist remains that have come to light at Kanchi. Much of the Buddhist heritage still remains unerathed at Kanchi, a part of which was known as Buddha Kanchi till atleast the fourteenth century.

2. Nagapattam

Nagapattam or Nagapattinam lies beyond Madras on the East Coast in Tanjore district of Tamil Nadu. This port city was a flourishing Buddhist centre for a long time. In the sixth century AD, the great Pali commentator, Dhammapala resided here in the *Dharmasoka Vihara*. This he mentions in the epilogue of his commentary on the *Netti-pakarana* which he composed while living in that Vihara. The Pallava king, Narasimhapotha-varman or Narasimhavarman II (c. 700-728 AD), constructed a *vihara*[51] at Nagapattam in 720 for the use of the Chinese mariners who frequented Nagapattam for purposes of trade. During the reign of the famous Chola king, Rajaraja (985-1040 AD), the Sailendra ruler of Sri Viajaya (Sumatra), built a Buddha *Vihara* at Nagapattam, which was called Siri Culamanivarama Cudamani *Vihara*[52] after the father of the ruler of Sri Vijaya. A copper plate inscription of the eleventh century states that the Chola king Rajaraja granted[53] the village of Anaigmangalam for the maintenance of the Buddhist shrine built by the Sailendra king Mara Vijayattungavarman of Sri Vijaya.

As late as the fourteenth century, the Chinese merchants called at Nagapattam for merchandise. An inscription engraved by them at the Chinese *Vihara* is known from the Chinese records. In the fifteenth century, a Burmese envoy consisting of eleven Burmese bhikkhus are said to have been sent by the Burmese king Ramapatiraja. On the way back, they were shipwrecked; reached Nagapattam and resided in the Chinese *Vihara*. This is confirmed by the Kalyani Sima rock inscription[54] in Burma.

A Buddhist structure was still standing at Nagapattam till 1867 when the Government of India permitted the Christian missionaries to demolish the same and erect a church instead. When the large tree near this gopuram, as it was then called, was being uprooted, five Buddha images were found. Four of them were of metal and one was of porcelain. When Lord Napier, the British Governor visited the place the missionaries presented these images to him. In the pedestal of one of the Buddha image, an inscription in Tamil was found. It read, "May it be auspicious! The Teacher to whom Agamama Panditar went for refuge for emancipation from Samsara".[55]

Nagapattam has also yielded a large number of bronze Buddha images. From 1856 onward, more than 350 bronze Buddhist images[56] some of them inscribed, have been discovered from the sites of the two *Viharas* built at Nagapattam by the Sailendra kings of Sri-Vijaya (Sumatra) during the reign of the Chola kings Rajaraja I and Rajendra Chola I. Some of these belong to the early Chola period (871-1070 AD) and a large number of them are of the later period (1070-1250 AD). A few large bronze Buddha images belonging to the sixteenth century have also been recovered from Nagapattam and other places in Tanjore district. Of these very late figures, important ones are 'the standing bronze Buddha figures enclosed within an elobarately worked prabhavali dated to about the 16th century AD and the Avalokitesvara image standing within a *prabhavali* dating from after 1600 AD'.[57] The existence of such large figures as these shows that Buddhism was a living faith in the district of Tanjore till the 17th century AD.

3. Buddhavedu

Buddhavedu is a small village 13 miles from Madras city. It is said that Lord Buddha rested here when He came to the South. Whatever may be truth in this legend, the archaeologists have since discovered here a rock inscription, a Buddha image, a Bodhi tree, and the remains of a Buddhist monastery.[58] The inscription reveals that this village had been dedicated to the

Buddhist *Sangha* during the reign of the Chola King, Rajaraja I in the tenth century AD.

4. Madras Museum

The Government Museum, Madras was established in 1851 and has the largest collection of Buddhist sculptures from Amaravati in Andhra Pradesh. This collection is largely of the sculptures discovered by James Burgess in 1881 and some sculptures discovered by Alaxendar Rea who excavated the site thrice in 1888-89, 1905-6 and 1908-9. These sculptures in marble and limestone cover a period of over 450 years from about BC 200 to AC 250. There are as many as 72 Amaravati sculptures depicting scenes from Buddha's Life, and 27 sculptures depicting Buddha's Previous Lives (Jatakas and Avadanas) in the Madras Museum. There are also a number of interesting Buddhist sculptures from Goli, Jaggayyapeta, Ghantasala and Bhattiprolu in Andhra Pradesh in this Museum. From within Tamil Nadu, the Buddha images from Kanchipuram, and Buddha images (in bronze) from Nagapattinam in district Tanjore are notable.

The period-wise distribution of Amaravati sculptures in the Madras Museum is as follows:[59]

First Period : c.a. 200 - 100 BC.

Four Scenes of this period are : 1. The shooting contest and other scenes; 2. The conversion of the Jatilas headed by Uruvlla Kassapa; 3. The story of Angulimala: The panel shows a fierce man with a sword, a flaming pillar surmounted by a trisula. A man is also kneeling near a pair of feet at the base of the pillar. A lady with a vessel on her head stands to the left of the pillar; and 4. Division of the Relics of the Buddha after the Maha-parinirvana at Kushinara.

Second Period : c.a. 100 AD.

Twenty scenes from Buddha's life of this period are : 1. The Dream of Maya; 2. The Temptation. 3. The Buddha and Nagas 4-6. The Bodhisattva's Departure, The Temptation and the attempted opening of the Ramagrama Stupa by Asoka. 7. The Ramagrama Stupa, 8. Symbolic representation of principal scenes of Buddha's life. 9-20 Symbolic representation of various scenes - adoration of the Bodhi tree, Dharmachakra, throne and flaming pillar etc. Of these, the first sculpture shows the dream of Maya of her bath in water from Anotatta lake. In the panel, five women with water jars are attending on a lady in the centre, standing at ease softly stroking her hair - she is taking a bath and arranging her toilet. The sculpture No. 3 shows nimbata Buddha seated on a low seat with his hands in Abhayamudra preaching to a nagaraja and nagini on either side of him. The nagaraja to his left has joined his hands in adoration, a nagini admires, and a deva flutters above with offerings. The sculpture No. 9 is a large slab showing Bodhi tree and empty throne on either side of which stand a man and woman of rank, all the four carrying vessels full of water. Devas flutter above carrying offerings, one on each side. There is a border of running lions at the top of this panel. To the right is a border with rail pillar pattern. The sculpture No. 15 is also a large slab showing Dharmachakra on a pillar behind empty throne adored by two noble looking devotees on each side, one standing waving a fly whisk and another seated with hands joined in reverence. A deva hovers above on either side with offerings.

Third Period : ca 150 AD.

Thirty one scenes of this period are; 1. Bodhisattva's Descent as a White Elephant, 2. Dream of Maya and its interpretation; 3. Suddhodana visits Maya in the Asoka Grove. 4. The Great Departure. 5. The Translation of the Bowl. 7. The Temptation. 8. The Great Enlightenment. 9. The First Sermon 10. The Conversion of Yasa and his friends. 11. The Conversion of the Bhaddhavaggiya Youths. 12. The Birth of Rahula and other scenes from Buddha's Life. 13. The Conversion of Nanda. 14. Sumana the Gardener, Sumana malakara. 15. Buddha subdues the fierce Elephant Nalagiri. 16. Ajatasatru visits Buddha. 17. A monkey offers honey to Buddha; 18. The story of Angulimala 19. The story of Angulimala repeated with slight variation. 20. Buddha performs a Miracle at Sravasti. 21. The Sravasti Miracle repeated with slight variation. 22. Buddha preaches to His Mother in Heaven. 23. King Pasendi (Prasenajit) entertains Ananda and other Monks. 24. Cullakara's wives regain their husband. 25. Rupananda learns of the Impermanence of Beauty. 26-27. The story of King Udayana and his Queens. 28. The Division of the Relics. 29. Symbolic Representation of Principal Scenes from Buddha's Life. 30. Stupa Adoration symbolising Buddha's Parinirvana. 31. Adoration of Buddha under the Bodhi Tree symbolising Englightenment. The sculpture (No. 2) depicts Dream of Maya and its Interpretation. It shows a king seated on a throne with his queen on a seat beside him attended by women with chauries in their hands. He is questioning others seated to his left. To the left is a royal lady on a couch guarded by four attendants, men and women. The sculpture No. 6 is a cross-bar showing the worship of Buddha's Alms Bowl. The scene is in the Tushita Heaven. A number of gods and goddesses are shown clustering round a bowl in a tray carried aloft and adored with great reverence. Nagas, garudas and other demigods dance while dwarf yakshas make soft music with conch and drum and divine damsels soar above with hands joined in adoration. The sculpture. No. 11 shows the conversation of the Bhaddhavaggiya youths by the Buddha. It is a cross-bar with empty throne and feet on footrest under Bodhi tree adored by thirty noble-looking turbaned youths, some standing waving chauries, others approaching or moving away with hands joined in adoration, yet others seated in the same attitude and some more reverently kneeling. The sculpture No. 15 shows Buddha subduing the fierce elephant Nalagari. The scene depicts the havoc caused by the mad elephant, Nalagari, let loose by Devadatta. The animal is shown rushing furiously along towards the Buddha and his monks in the streets of Rajagrha. The people are painstricken at the sight of the mad elephant. Those that have entered their houses watch from their balconies with reverence and pity. Then at the right end the elephant is shown kneeling before the Buddha. The Buddha has been shown here in the form of a flaming pillar above a pair of feet on a lotus. The sculpture No. 28 is a coping stone carved on both sides. The inner side shows seven elephants with two riders each, one holding a casket, and another waving a chauri, issuing from a city gateway within which in three panels two scenes of important discussion and consultation among chiefs, and one of musical and dance festivities are shown. The sculpture No. 30 depicts Buddha's Parinirvana. This is a cross-bar with medallion representing the worship of the stupa. A man and woman are kneeling in the foreground before the stupa. To the right are five men, two playing drum and others the flute, and to the left are six women and two boys reverently approaching, one of them carrying a tray with offerings.

The Jatakas depicted in the Amaravati sculptures of this period are : 1. The Snake charmer and his Monkey, Ahigundika Jataka, 2. The story of Bhuridatta, Bhuridatta Jataka, 3. The Noble Six-tusked Elephant, Chhaddanta Jataka, 4. The Love-smitten King, Culabodhi Jataka, 5 & 6. The Wicked King who chopped his son into bits, Culladhammapala Jataka. 7. The Story of Messenger, Duta Jataka. 8. Mara obstructs Pacceka Buddha's Feeding, Khadirangara Jataka. 9. The Elephant Mahilamukha is taught Virtue, Mahilamukha Jataka. 10. The Story of Mittavaindaka the Unfortunate One, Losaka Jataka. 11. The Story of Matanga, Matanga Jataka. 12. The Story of the Virtuous Prince, Mahapadama Jataka. 13. The Peacock preaches the Dhamma, Mora Jataka. 14. The Story of Prince Somanassa, Somanassa Jataka. 15 & 16. Virtue rewarded, Suruci Jataka. 17. The Presents of King Bandhuma; introduction to Vessantara Jataka. 18-20. Vidhura the Wise One, Vidhurapandita Jataka.

Other scenes from Buddha's Previous Lives are:

1. Ghoshaka the Fortunate, Ghoshakasetthi Uppatti. 2. The Story of Kavikumara, Kavikumaravada, 3. Mandhata, the Universal Monarch. 4. Saka gains a Celestial Nymph Rohin Khattiyakanna. 5. The Story of Sarvambad, Sarvamdadavadana.

Fourth Period : ca 200-250 AD.

Seventeen scenes of Buddha's life of this period are:

1. Maya's Dream and its Interpretation. 2. The Miracle under the Jambu tree at Kapilavastu. 3. The Renunciation. 4. Scenes ending with Mara's claim of Bodhisattva's seat. 5. Sujata feeds the Bodhisattva - the slab slightly broken shows Buddha (Headless) seated on a throne and women attending on him with great devotion while some are requesting him to partake of food brought by them. 6. The Temptation. 7-8. The Conversion of Nanda. 9. Rahula asks for his inheritence - the sculpture shows Rahula being brought near Buddha and urged to ask for his inheritence, Buddha who is shown here with a halo, is leaving the palace. Rahula's mother and her companions are respectively standing aside, watching the boy as he approaches his father. 10. Principal scenes from Buddha's Life. 11-16. Some more scenes from Buddha's Life. 17. The Stupa of Ramagrama.

There are only two scenes from Buddha's Previous Lives. These are : Vessantara the Generous Prince, Vessantara Jataka and the Stories of Sarvamdada and Vidhurapandita.

Besides the Amaravati sculptures, there are a number of interesting Buddhist sculptures from Goli, Jaggyyapeta, Ghantasala and Bhattiprolu in Andhra Pradesh in this Museum. From within Tamil Nadu, the Buddha images from Kanchipuram, and Buddha's images (in bronze) from Nagapattam in district Tanjore are notable.

(IV) THE BUDDHIST LEGACY

Kanchipuram, the first and foremost citadal of Buddhism in Tamil Nadu, has yielded a number of remarkable Buddha images. And their discovery in some cases from the innermost parts of the temples goes to show that the present day Hindu temples are either converted and re-adopted Buddhist shrines or are built with the material from the Buddha Viharas. According to T.A. Gopinatha Rao, who discovered in 1915 five Buddha images from inside the *Kamakshi Amman* temple at Kanchi, the present Hindu temple was originally a Buddhist shrine dedicated to the goddess Tara.[60] Like the *Kamakshi Amman kovil*, the *Karukkilamarnda Amman kovil* and the *Ekamersvara kovil* are also converted Buddhist shrines. Similarly, the *Darupadiyamman kovil*, the *Dharmaraja kovil*, and the *Vinayaka kovil* were also earlier Buddhist shrines.

What we see at Kanchipuram, may also be true of other Buddhist shrines elsewhere in Tamil Nadu. The religion of the Buddha is said to have been ousted from the Tamil land by the *Alvars* (Vaishnava) and *Nayanaras* (Saiva) saints who popularised the Bhakti cult in South India during the period from seventh century to ninth century. It is claimed that the Buddhist scholars were worsted by them in debates, wordy duels. But more than that, violent reaction against Buddhism and persecution of Buddhists by them seems to be responsible for the final eclipse of Buddhism from Tamil Nadu. Dr. N. Subramanian rightly observes[61]: "It is commonly said that there was no religious persecution among the Hindus. This is too tall a claim; for one thing it is not natural for adherents of one religion to totally `tolerate' the followers of other sects... for another we have positive evidence of sectarian feuds; the Saiva opposition to the Jainas and Bauddhas illustrated by the lives of Appar and Sambandar and all that happened in Kanchi and Madurai in that context may be considered the first chapter of this rather inglorious tradition of inter-denominational feuds".

That even the Buddhist shrines were robbed of gold and other valuables is evident from the story of a robber turned saint, Tirumangai Alvar who lived in the eighth century. According to Nilakanta Sastri[62]: "Tirumangai Alvar was the petty chieftain of Alinadu in Tanjore district who, legend says, became a highway man in order to carry off and marry the daughter of a Vaishnavite doctor of higher caste, for whom he also changed his religion. He is said to have stolen a solid golden image of Buddha from a monastery in Nagapattam to pay for renovating the temple of Srirangam..... His hymns, and they are many, are equally full of attacks on Jainism and Buddhism..."

The legacy of Buddhism also survives in the worship of the Bodhi tree in South India. It is significant that the Shaivite teachers like Appar, Sundarar, Tirugnana-sambandhar in their *Theravam* hymns refer to the Buddhists as *'bodhiyar'* or worshippers of the Bodhi-tree, the sacred tree sitting under which Lord Buddha had attained enlightenment. A Jaina work *Nilakesi* in Tamil also refers to the Buddhists as worshippers of the Bodhi tree.

The richest Buddhist legacy is in the Tamil literature.[63] It may look strange yet it is a fact that out of the five celebrated Epics in Tamil language, namely, *Siilappadikaram, Manimekhalai, Valaiyapathy, Kundalakesi,* and *Jivaka Cintamani,* three are the works of Buddhist poets. These are : *Manimekhalai, Valaipathy* and *Kundalakesi.* The remaining two works, *Silappadikaram* and *Jivaka-Cintamani* are by the Jaina poets. Of the three Buddhist epics, only the epic *Manimekhalai* has come to us; the other two having been lost during the time when Buddhism fell on bad days. Both the Jaina epics have, however, survived.

In the Tamil classic, *Manimekhalai,* the poet Sittlai Sattanar, besides telling the story of the Buddhist nun, gives a graphic picture of political, social and religious conditions prevalent in the Chera, Chola and Pandya kingdoms of those days. Further, he not only highlights the fundamentals of Buddhism but also discusses the other religious and philosophical systems prevalent in South India in the second century AD.

The second Buddhist epic, *Kundalakesi,* was written by another eminent poet, Nagaguttanar, who lived in the fourth century AD. In this poem, the author had made a comparative evaluation of the Buddhist philosophy with the Vedic and Jaina philosophies. Unfortunately, this work has been lost but a large number of quotations from it are found in the books by other authors, in particular, in *Nilakesi,* written by a Jaina poet in reply to *Kundalakesi.*

The third Tamil epic written by a Buddhist poet, *Valiyapathy,* has also been lost. However, quotations from it are found in other literary works.

Two other Tamil works by Buddhist authors were *Siddhatattokai* and *Tiruppadigam*, the former a work on the Buddhist philosophy, and the latter containing devotional hymns in praise of the Buddha. Both these works have also been lost but their existence is confirmed by the quotations from them given by Ghanaprakasar, author of a paraphrase of a religious Shaiva book named*"Sivanagana-Siddhyar"* and by the author of a paraphrase of the Jaina work *`Nilakesi'*.

Yet another Tamil work by a Buddhist author was *Bimbisara Kadai*, narrating the story of King Bimbisara of Magadha, who was contemporary of the Buddha. This work is also lost but the Hindu scholar Ganaprakasar quotes verses from it and acknowledges the source.

The last eminent Buddhist scholar of Tamil language was Buddhamitra who flourished in the eleventh century. He wrote a Tamil grammer, at the request of the Chola King Virarajendra, and named the work after his royal patron as *'Virasoliyam'*. This work still survives, and its importance lies in the fact that this pioneer work, wherein Buddhamitra had introduced Sanskrit norms into Tamil grammer, was followed[64] devoutly by grammarians like Senavaraiyar, Isandesigar,Sivananamunivar and Subrahmania Dikshitar in later times.

As for the Buddhist influence on Hindu thought, the Advaita-vada or Vedanta of Sankaracharya (788-820 AD) is largely a modified version of the Sunyavada of Nagarjuna. As says Dr. Das Gupta,[65] "a careful analysis of Sankara's writings demonstrates indisputably that he largely borrowed his doctrine, his phraseology, his dilectics and his method of approach from Buddhism. Not only he but many of his followers like Sriharsa, Anandjnana and others who constructed the Vedanta into a rational system of philosophy deliberately followed the foot prints of Nagarjuna and other Buddhist writers". Another scholar says[66]: "Sankara was tremendously influenced by Buddhism - in fact he was described by his opponents as crypto - Buddhist. Although Sankara has criticised Buddhist subjective idealism

(Vijnanavada or Yogacara) and absolute nihilism (Sunyavada or Madhyamika), his own view is not very different from that of the Yogacara school which insists on the existence of pure consciousness as the only reality. This pure consciousness of the Yogacara school is the same as the *brahman* of Sankara." In South India, two Hindu opponents of Sankara were Ramanuja (1018-1137 AD), and Madhvacharya (1198-1275 AD). Both are critical of him. While Ramanuja called Sankara's Vedanta "hidden Buddhism", Madhvacharya refuted Sankara's philosophy saying it was Buddhism in a different garb.

In the Pali literature there is an anthology of 423 select sayings of the Buddha contained in the most popular and famous Buddhist scripture 'Dhammapada'. The *Dhammapada* has been acclaimed as the best companion and never failing guide for every one in all times and claims. There is a similar classic named *Tirukkural* or *Kural* in Tamil literature also. Written by the poet Thiruvalluvar, this classic has 130 sections of 10 couplets each covering the whole range of human existence. Like the Dhammapada, it is comprehensive in scope and cosmopolitan in its appeal. It seems that the author of Kural was aware of the Dhammapada and may have drawn inspiration from the sayings of the Buddha for his work. A comparative study[8] made by Dr. B.C. Law[67] in 1942 shows remarkable resemblence between the teachings of the Buddha as contained in the Dhammapada and the Tirukkural.

(V) THE REVIVAL MOVEMENT

The Buddhist revival movement began in Tamil Nadu almost simultaneously with the revival movement in North India. With the establishment of the head office of the Theosophical Society in India at Adyar, Madras, Colonel H.S. Olcott became a frequent visitor to Madras. Since he had embraced Buddhism in Ceylon, which had attracted world-wide attention, the Untouchables, the Panchamas as they were called in South India were also attracted towards Buddhism. When in June 1898, Col. Olcott and Anagarika

Dharmapala visited Adyar, a delegation of the Panchamas met them and sought admission to Buddhism. Dharmapala in his diary jottings for 4 June 1898 records; "The Panchamas, descendents of ancient Buddhists, called on Colonel to present their petition to admit them as Buddhists". Dharmapala further records on 7 June, "In the evening the Panchama meeting held in Raypettah. Col. Olcott and the old priest and myself represented the Buddhists. An intelligent body of men they were. Buddha's Dhamma is above caste and the Panchamas will be raised from their degraded condition and the influence of the Dhamma shown."

These Panchamas or the Untouchables were led by an enlightened person, Pandit Ayodhya Dasa or Ayoti Dasa. He was the first person to embrace Buddhism in 1898 itself. In order to give practical shape to his idea - to gain freedom from slavery and serfdom, to cast away Hinduism in which there was nothing for the Panchamas except hatred, abhorrence and humiliation, Pandit Ayodhya Dasa founded in 1900 the South India Buddhist Association at Perambur, Madras. This Association is still holding aloft the banner of the *Dhamma* in the South. Pandit Ayodhya Dasa wrote an important work in Tamil titled *'Buddharadam Adivedam'*. He also edited for a number of years the Weekly Tamil Bulletin *'Tamlian'* on behalf of the South India Buddhist Association, which ceased publication few years after his demise in 1914.

Another pioneer Buddhist leader of South India was Appadorai or Appaswami. He was one of the many untouchable Tamils who found work in the Kolar Gold Fields (now in Karnataka), and it was he who created a strong Buddhist base at Kolar Gold Fields in the 1920's. Even today, K.G.F. is a Buddhist centre. Amongst the scholars who took interest in Buddhism, mention may be made of A.S. Mudaliyar who published a small pamphlet on Buddhism in 1903; S. Krishnaswami Aiyangar, V.R. Ramachandra Dikshitar, H.R. Rangaswamy, T.N. Ramachandran, N. Aiyaswami Sastri and K.R. Subramanian.

One of the most eminent Buddhist scholars produced by modern South India was Prof. P. Lakshmi Narasu. Prof. Narasu was a graduate in Physics from the Madras Christian College, In 1897, he was appointed as Assistant Professor of Physics and Chemistry at the same College. His eminence as an Educationist was recognised soon, and before long he was appointed as Principal of the Pachiappa's College.

Prof. Narasu was known to Anagarika Dharmapala, founder of the Maha Bodhi Society of India. In the year 1900, he, together with M. Singaravelu opened a branch of the Maha Bodhi Society in Madras. He also managed for sometime, on behalf of the Maha Bodhi Society, a school hall at Perambur, Madras for the elementary education of "Dravidian Buddhist children". Being more interested in the revival of Buddhism in practical terms, he later actively collaborated with the South India Buddhist Association, of which he became President, after the demise of Pandit Ayodhya Dasa, its founder.

Prof. Narasu was a prolific writer and logician. His book 'The Essence of Buddhism' which was first published in 1907, again in 1912 is by any standard the best book on Buddhism and comparative study of other religions. His command over the subject and the language is marvellous. At one place, he says; "Dogma and miracle are wisdom to the Christians; kismet and fanaticism are wisdom to the Moslem; caste and ceremonialism are wisdom to the Brahmin; asceticism and nakedness are wisdom to the Jain; mysticism and magic are wisdom to the Taoist; formalism and outward piety are wisdom to the Confucian; ancestor-worship and loyality to the Mikado are wisdom to the Shintoist; but love and piety are the first wisdom to the Buddhist".

Dr. B.R. Ambedkar liked Prof. Narasu's book so much that he recommended it for study to his followers, and himself wrote a Preface, giving a brief life-sketch of the author, while getting its third edition published in 1948. Dr. Ambedkar hailed Prof. Narasu as "a prodigy of the last century", and paid tribute to him in the following words:

"Prof. Narasu was the stalwart of the 19th century who had fought European arrogance with patriotic fervour, orthodox Hinduism with inconoclastic zeal, heterodox Brahmins with nationalistic vision and aggressive Christianity with a rationalistic outlook - all under the inspiring banner of his unflagging faith in the teachings of the Great Buddha".

Prof. Narasu wrote another popular book 'What is Buddhism' which serves as a brief but 'very useful' introduction to Buddhism.

Professor Lakshmi Narasu passed away in 1934.

The first Buddha *Vihara* to be built in Tamil Nadu was by the South India Buddhist Association at Perambur. Known as Mrs. Mary Foster's Buddhist Hall (41 Paddy Field Road, Perambur Madras), it was purchased largely with the funds donated by Mrs. Mary, E. Foster of Honolulu, who collaborated with Anagarika Dharamapala and invested in India. The first Bhikkhu-in-charge of this *Vihara* was Bhikkhu Nandarama of Sri Lanka who came in 1906 and preached *Dhamma* amongst the local people. The Buddhist Hall to this day remains the headquarters of the South India Buddhist Association.

One of the most prominent Buddhist monks to propagate *Dhamma* in the Tamil land was Ven. Nilwakke Somananda Thera, a Tamil knowing monk, who was for a time in the 1930's representative of the Maha Bodhi Society in Madras. Another notable Bhikkhu to work in this State was Ven. E. Nandiswara who was Bhikkhu-in-charge of the Maha Bodhi Society, Madras for more than 15 years from 1970 onward. At present the chief Incumbent of the Buddha *Vihara* at Kennet Lane, Egmore, Madras is Ven. U. Ratanapala. He is quite active and moves in the whole of South India.

Two other *Viharas* in Tamil Nadu are at Buddhavedu, district Madras, and Rajapalayam, district Ramnad. In spite of the best efforts of the Buddhist savants, the population of Buddhists in this State has not increased much. In 1981, there were only 735 Buddhists in Tamil Nadu.

Notes and References

1. British Museum Plates of Charudevi.
2. K.A. Nilakanta Sastri, History of South India, Madras, 1984, p. 144.
3. S. Krishnaswami Aiyangar, History of Tirupati, Vol. I, p. 5.
4. S. Krishnaswami Aiyangar, in his introduction to R. Gopalan's History of Pallavas of Kanchi, Madras, 1928.
5. R. Sathianata Aiyer, HCIP, Vol. III, p. 266.
6. Nilakanta Sastri, History of South India, p. 144.
7. The Original in Pali is as follows:
   'Buddhassa Buddhasehene Vinayasa Vaniccayo
   Buddha-siham Samuddossa Mamasati Viharim
   Kodayam Bana Bikkonam Hidattaya Samasado
   Vijayassava Porrandum Sukena Vasiranesa
   Accuta Vikkante Kalappa Kulanadane
   Mahimsamanu Sasande Aratto Sa-sampito'.
8. Yapparungala Virutti, Bhavandam Pillai 1916, p. 293. - quoted by V. Ramamurthy, History of Kongu, Madras, 1986, p. 151.
9. Nilakanta Sastri, History of South India, p. 145.
10. T.N. Ramachandran, Nagapattinam and other Buddhist Bronzes, Madras 1934, p. 14 H. Dhammaratana Thera, Buddhism in South India, Kandy, Sri Lanka, 1968, p. 12.
11. Nilakanta Sastri, History of South India, p. 437.
12. Ibid. p. 182.
13. Ibid. p. 191.
14. P.R. Srinivasan, Story of Buddhism with Special Reference to South India, Madras, 1960, p. xi.
15. H. Dhammaratana Thera, Buddhism in South India, Buddhist Publication Society, Kandy, Ceylon, 1968, p. 22.
16. Ibid., p. 34.
17. Ibid., p. 34.

18. P.R. Srinivasan, Ed., Story of Buddhism with Special Reference to South India, Madras, 1960, p. 30.
19. Manimekhalai, Chapter XXX, Translated by Rao Bahadur Krishnaswami Aiyangar, 1928 - Reproduced from Buddhism in South India, H. Dhammaratana Thera, p. 60.
20. The Vinaya sub-commentary named 'Vimativinodani' in Pali by Kassapa Thera (12th century) refers to Kundalakesi as a work by Nagasena, as under : "Formerly in this Tamil country an elder named Nagasena compiled in Tamil containing the story of Kundalakshi, for refuting heretical doctrines adducing arguments for demolishing the views advanced by non-Buddhists". The name Nagaguttanar may be the Tamilised version of the name Nagasena.
21. Uragapura has been identified with modern Uraiyur situated on the southern bank of the river Kaveri.
22. Cf. V. Ramamurthy, History of Kongu, Madras, 1986, p. 151.
23. Mahavamsa, XXXVII, pp. 225-230.
24. Story of Buddhism, p. 158: C.R. Srinivasan, Kanchipuram Through the Ages, p. 233.
25. P.V. Bapat Ed. 2500 Years of Buddhism, Delhi, 1987 edition, p. 189.
26. Ibid.
27. The colophon in Pali reads as follows.
"Saddhammotaratthane
Pasttane naga savhaya
Dhammasoka Maharaja
Vihare vasata maya."
The Sasanvamsa, a Chronicle of Sri Lanka, refers to Dhammapala as follows : "Acharya Dhammapala, who compiled a number of commentaries such as the one on the Itivuttaka, was a resident of the Badarittha Vihara in the Tamil country". Cf. H. Dhammaratana Thera, Buddhism in South India, p. 41.
28. Taranatha's History of Buddhism in India, translated into the Tibetan by Lama Chimpa and Alaka Chattopadhaya edited by Debiprasad Chasttopadhyay, Calcutta, 1980, p. 181.

29 . P.C. Bagchi, India and China, pp. 107-109.

30 . 2500 Years of Buddhism, 1956, p. 245.

31 . Samuel Beal, Buddhist Records of the Western World, Delhi, 1980. edition, p. 229.

32 . 2500 Years of Buddhism, p. 225. Taranatha's History of Buddhism in India, p. 228.

33 . Dalsukh Malvania on Dharmakirti in "Seers and Thinkers", Publications Division, Delhi, 1979, pp. 65-75.

34 . D.C. Ahir, Heritage of Buddhism, Delhi, 1989, p. 85.

35 . H. Dhammaratana Thera, Buddhism in South India,p. 42.

36 . Shiego Kanata, Cultural Exchange between India, China and Japan - Imprints of Indian Thought and Culture Abroad, Vivekananda Kendra Patrika, Madras, Volume, 9, No.1, Febturay, 1980, pp. 95-97.

37 . H. Dhammaratana Thera, Buddhism in South India, pp. 42-43.

38 . Ibid., p. 44.

39 . Ibid., p. 43.

40 . Ibid., p. 44.

41 . IIbid., p. 44.

42 . Samuel Beal, Buddhist Records of the Western World, 1980 edition, Delhi, 1980 edition, p. 228.

43 . 2500 Years of Buddhism, 1987 edition p. 296.

44 . C.R. Srinivasan, Kanchipuram Through the Ages, p. 238.

45 . Ibid.

46 . Buddhist Vestiges in Kanchipuram, cf. Story of Buddhism, p. 71.

47 . Story of Buddhism, p. 72.

48 . Ibid., p. 93. pp. 98-99.

49 . Ibid. p. 100.

50 . Ibid. p. 93.

51 . H. Dhammaratana Thera, Buddhism in South India, 1968, p. 12.

52 . K.A. Nilakanta Sastri, History of South India, p. 182.

53. P.V. Bapat, 2500 Years of Buddhism, p. 295.

54. H. Dhammaratana Thera, Buddhism in South India, p. 13.

55. Ibid.

56. 2500 Years of Buddhism, p. 252.

57. Story of Buddhism, p. 101.

58. D.C. Ahir, India's Debt to Buddhism, New Delhi. 1964, p. 88

59. C. Sivaramamurti, Amaravati Sculptures in the Madras Museum, Government Museum, Madras, 1977, pp. 151-270. First Period, pp. 151-164. Second Period, pp. 164-174. Third Period, pp. 175-248. Fourth Period, pp. 248-270.

60. Elements of Hindu Iconography, Madras 1924, Cf. C.R. Srinivasan, Kanchipuram Through the Ages, Delhi, 1979, p. 269.

61. N. Subramanian, History of Tamilnad, Madurai, 1972, p. 385.

62. K.A. Nilakanta Sastri, History of South India, Madras, 1984 edition, p. 426.

63. H. Dhammaratana Thera, Buddhism in South India, Kandy, Sri Lanka, 1968, pp. 23-30.

64. N. Subramanian, History of Tamilnad, p. 374.

65. Surrendranath Dasgupta, Maha Bodhi Journal, Calcutta, 1931, p. 552.

66. N.N. Bhattacharya, Ancient History of Civilization, New Delhi, 1988, pp. 242-243.

67. B.C. Law, Indological Studies, Part II, The Indian Research Institute, Calcutta, 1942, pp. 303-321.

APPENDIX I

EXTRACT
From
Manimekhalai in its Historical Setting

by
Dr. S. Krishnaswami Aiyangar
Luzac & Co. Ltd., London, 1928.

MANIMEKHALAI

BOOK XXX

Manimēkhalai who had already learned all that had happened in her previous birth, after having taken upon herself the duty of giving gifts (dāna) after walking in the path of right conduct (sila) worshipped three times the triple jewel of Buddha, Dhamma and Sangha, placing herself entirely under its protection, and then saluted the bhikkhu Aravana Adigal. The bhikkhu, in expounding to her the righteous path of the Dhamma, said:

"At that time when the world was full of beings poor in understanding, the Buddha, at the earnest entreaty of all the celestial beings of Tushitaloka, appeared on earth, leaving that heaven of joy empty. Then, seated at the foot of the Bodhi tree he conqured the enemy Māra and became the Victor (jina). The good teaching of the Four Truths which the beautiful victor imparted after having pulled out by the roots the three faults[1], were taught with ineffable beneficence in the past by innumerable other Buddhas. These Truths provide the means of crossing the ocean of existence by destroying the twelve Nidanas[2]. These latter appear one from the other in order as cause and effect and being capable of reappearance, (each link) as consequent upon that which is before it, assume the form of a never-ending circle. When in this order of cause and consequence the first ceases to exist, the next follows in cessation; when it comes into existence, that which follows it does so inevitably. So these are properly described as a chain of causes and conditions. Thus arranged these twelve Nidanas fall into four divisions[3], showing three joints[4]. Appearance in birth or rebirth is of three kinds (human, heavenly or of the nether world), and is of three divisions in time, past present and future[5]. These also produce the faults, deeds and their consequences[6], and are impermanent and cause only sorrow. He who gets to understand this character of these Nidanas, he knows what will assure him the permanence of release (Nirvana).

"Further, it becomes the means for the cultivation of the Four Truths[7], and is constituted of the five Skandhas. It is capable of being argued in the six forms beginning with the 'assertion of truth'[8]. It results in the four forms of excellence. It is open to question in four ways and being capable of respective answers in four ways similarly. It is without origin and without end. It is a series of continuous becoming without ever reaching final destruction. It neither does, nor can it be described as being done. It is neither self nor is it possessed by another self. It is nothing that is gone, nothing that is to come. It cannot be brought to an end, nor is it to end itself. It is itself the result of the deed, birth and cessation. Such is the nature of the twelve causes and conditions beginning with ignorance, and called the Nidanas. These twelve are:

(1) Ignorance (*Pedamai,* Sans. *Avidyā*),

(2) Action (*Seykai,* Sans. *Karma*),

(3) Consciousness (*Uṇarvu,* Sans. *Vijñāna*),

(4) Name and Form (*Aru-uru,* Sans. *Nāmarūpa*).

(5) Six organs of sense (*Vāyil,* Sans. *Saḍayatanā*)

(6) Contact (*Uru,* Sans. *Sparsa*),

(7) Sensation (*Nuharvu,* Sans. *Vedanā*),

(8) Thirst or Craving (*Vetkai,* Sans. *Tṛṣna*),

(9) Attachment (*Parru,* Sans. *Upādāna*),

(10) Becoming or existence (*Pavam,* Sans. *Bhava*),

(11) Birth (*Torram,* Sans. *Jāti*),

(12) The result of action, old age and death (*Vinayppayan,* Sans. *Jarā-maraṇa*).

"If people understand the twelvefold nature of the chain of cause and effect, they then understand the supreme truth and will enjoy permanent bliss. If they do not, they are bound to suffer in the depths of hell.

(1) Ignorance consists in not understanding what was explained above, in being liable to delusion and in believing in what one hears to the neglect of that which one is able to see for himself, as believing in the existence of the horns of a rabbit because someone else says that they do exist.

(2) In the three world, life is illimitable, and living beings in them are of six classes. They are men, gods, brahmas, the inhabitants of hell, the crowd of animals and spirits. According to good deeds and bad, life takes its birth in one or other of these. Ever since it assumes the form of embryo, the result of these deeds will show themselves either in the happiness of mind or in anxiety of suffering. Of these evil deeds - killing, theft and illicit sexual behaviour show themselves as evils springing up in the body. Lying, speaking ill of others, harsh words, and useless talk, these four show themselves as evils of speech. Desire, anger and illusion are three evils that arise in the mind[9]. These ten the wise would avoid. If they should fail to do so, they would be born as animals or spirits or beings of the nether world, and make themselves liable to extreme anxiety of mind and

suffering. Good men, on the contrary, would avoid these ten, and assuming the good discipline (silam) and taking upon themselves to do deeds of charity (danam), will be born in the three higher classes of beings, such as devas (gods), men or Brahmas, and live a life of enjoyment and happiness as a result of good deeds.

(3) Consciousness (Unarvu) consists in feeling like one asleep, without the feeling leading to any action, or to any satisfaction[10].

(4) Name and form consist in that which has the feeling described above, and constituting mind and body.

(5) Organs of sense are, on examination, those that carry consciousness to the mind (Vijñāna or Ullam).

(6) Contact consists in Vijñāna and the organs of sense experiencing touch with other things (veru pulangal).

(7) Sensation (Nuharvu) consists in the mind or Vijñāna enjoying that of which it has become conscious.

(8) Thirst or craving consists in not feeling satisfied with that which is thus enjoyed.

(9) Attachment consists in the desire for enjoyment impelling one into action.

(10) Becoming consists in the accumulation of deeds indicating the consequence to which each leads[11].

(11) Birth (Tonral) consists in the result of deeds leading to the conscious taking of birth in one or other of the six forms of birth in the inevitable chain of cause and effect.

(12) Disease (Piṇi) consists in the suffering of the body by a change from its natural condition in consequence of the result of deeds. Old age (Mūppu) consists in the loosening the body as one draws nearer and nearer to the end. Death (Sākkaāḍu) ultimately consists in the human body, composed of life and body, disappearing as the setting sun.

"From ignorance arises action; from action springs consciousness; from consciousness come name and form;[12] from name and from spring the organs of sense; through organs of sense contact becomes possible; contact results in sensation or experience; experience produces desire; from desire springs attachment; from attachment comes into existence collection of deeds; as a result of this collective deed arise various other forms of birth; birth inevitably brings along with it age, disease and death, and the consequent anxiety and the feeling of incapacity to get rid of it. This never-ending suffering is the ultimate result.

In such a never-ending circle of experience, when ignorance ceases, action will cease; with action consciousness will cease; with consciousness name and form (mind and body) will cease; with the cessation of name and form, organs of sense will cease; with the cessation of the organs of sense, contact will cease; contact ceasing, sensation or experience will cease; with sensation or experience ceasing desire will cease, desire ceasing to exist, there will be no attachment; without attachment, there is no accumulation of deeds; without the accumulated mass of deeds, there will be no becoming; with the cessation of becoming, there will be no birth, no disease, no age, no death, and in consequence, no anxiety and no helplessness. Thus, this never-ending series of suffering will be destroyed.

Of these twelve Nidanas, the first two, ignorance and action, are regarded as belonging to the first section. All those that follow spring from these two. The following five, namely, name and form, organs of sense, contact, experience, these five, as springing from the former two, are regarded as constituting the second division. Thirst, attachment and the collection of deeds constitute the third division as the result as evil in the enjoyment of the previous five, and, in consequence, as action resulting therefrom. It is from the folly of desire and consequent attachment that becoming arises. The fourth division includes birth, disease, age and death, since these four are experienced as a result of birth.[13]

Action is the cause of birth and consciousness springs out of it, where these two meet they mark the first conjunction. Where sensation and craving meet, it marks the second conjunction. The third junction comes in where the accumulation of deeds results in birth. Thus are marked the three points of junction in this chain of twelve causes and conditions.

The three forms of birth are those of men, gods and animals. These result from the consciousness in previous birth as a result of the conformations springing out of ignorance. This happens either from the delusion that this kind of birth is actually cessation of birth or the taking of birth in a new form without the consciousness, or the new birth coming with consciousness and the new form existing together. The three times are the past, present and future. Of these the past includes ignorance and action. To the present refer consciousness, name and form, the organs of sense, contact, sensation, thirst (or craving), the becoming and birth. To the future belong birth, disease, age and death. The resulting anxiety and helplessness are evils that spring out of the previous series of present action.

Desire, attachment and ignorance, these and the birth resulting therefrom constitute action in the present and cause future birth. Consciousness, a name and form, organs of sense, contact, sensation (or experience), birth, age, disease and death, these are the consequential experience in life, both present and future. These are full of evil, of deeds, and of consequences resulting from these deeds, and thus constitute suffering. Being such, they are all impermanent. While the nature of release (Vīḍu) consists in the understanding that there is nothing like a soul in anything existing.

Consciousness, name and form, the organs of sense, contact, sensation, birth, disease, age, and death, with the resulting anxiety and helplessness, these constitute disease. For this disease the causes are ignorance, action, desire, attachment and the collection of deeds. For suffering and birth, attachment is the cause; for bliss and cessation of birth, non-attachment is the cause. Words that embody this idea constitute the 'Four Truths', namely, suffering, the cause of suffering, removal of suffering, and the way to remove suffering.

Bondage and release result from the Skandhas (the aggregates of things). There is no agent outside entitled to bring them into contact. For the Skandhas and their manifestations as described above, the cause is the group of three evils: desire, anger and illusion.

Examine separately and understand that everything is impermanent, full of suffering, without a soul and unclean; thus treating it, give up desire! Realizing that friendliness, compassion and joy (at the well-being of others) constitute the best attitude of mind, give up anger! By the practice of hearing (sruti), mentation (cintana), experiencing in mind (bhavana) and realizing in vision (darsana), reflect, realize and give up all illusion! In these four ways get rid of the darkness of mind!"

In these auspicious words, free from inconsistency, (Aravana Adigal) exhibited the illuminating lamp of knowledge. Manimekhalai having assumed the habit of an ascetic (tapasi) and having heard the excellent exposition of the Dharma, devoted herself to penance[14] that she may get rid of the bondage of birth.

ACKNOWLEDGEMENT

Reproduced from the Appendix to Buddhism in South India, by Ven. Hisselle Dhammaratana Mahathera, Buddhist Publication Society, Kandy, Sri Lanka, 1968 - The Wheel Publication No. 124/125. The Notes and References were added by the Editor of 'The Wheel' series.

Notes and References

1. The three Roots of Evil (akusala-mula): greed, hate and delusion.
2. The twelve links of the Dependent Origination (paticcasamuppāda).
3. The four sections (Cattāro sangaha), see Visuddhi Magga (tr. by Nyanamoli), Ch XVII, $ 290.
4. The three joints (ti-sandhi), see Vis M XVII, $ 289.
5. See VisM. XVII, $ 287.
6. See in VisM. XVII, & 298 the threefold Round' (ti-vaṭṭa) of defilements (kilesa), kammic action (kamma) and kamma-result (vipaka).
7. See VixM. XVII $ 300.
8. "Six Forms", see ib., $ 299
9. These are the'ten unwholesome courses of action' (dasa akusla kamma-patha).
10. This might be a reference to the definition of Consciousness, in this context, as Rebirth Consciousness (patisandhi citta) which is a kind of subliminal consciousness (bhavanga citta).
11. This refers to a twofold division of Becoming (bhava), the Kamma-process (kamma-bhava) and the Rebirth-process (upapatti-bhava).
12. i.e. mind and body.
13. See Vism XVII, $290.
14. Nottal; better to be translated by "religious life".

APPENDIX II

Tirukkuṛaḷ And Dhammapada A Comparative Study

by
Dr. B.C. Law

Indological Studies - Part II
The Indian Research Institute Calcutta, 1942

(Page 303-321)

TIRUKKURAL AND DHAMMAPADA - A COMPARATIVE STUDY

The Tamil text of the Tirukkuṛaḷ of Tiruvaḷḷuvar is regarded as one of the holy scriptures by the Tamilians like the Bhagavadgita of the Hindus and the Dhammapada of the Buddhists. It consists of three parts, the first dealing with Aram, the second with Poral and the last with Kāma. It really treats of Dharma, Artha, and Kama. The probable date of its composition is the first or second century B.C. This important text, which is considered as the Tamil classic, contains invaluable moral teachings. Prof, Dikshitar of the Madras University has quite recently translated it into English with the Tamil text transcribed in Roman script for the Adyar Library series. The Dhammapada which is the second book of the Khuddakanikaya of the Suttapiṭaka contains the sublime teachings of the Buddha. The verses are compiled from various sources and nowhere do we find any mention of the authorship of each of the verses. They are mostly detached. The majority of them is found in other canonical texts. There are various recensions, and different editions and translations. It is highly esteemed in Ceylon as a classical work. It is really indispensable to students of Buddhism.

An attempt has been made here to bring to the notice of the readers the teachings common to both the text of the Tirukkuṟaḷ and Dhammapada.

According to the Tirukkural[1] those who have attained the feet of the Lord, will be free from all troubles. Those who have sought refuge in the feet of the Lord, can shake off anxiety, and those who have gained the feet of the Lord, cross the ocean of births.

According to the Dhammapada[2] he who takes refuge in the Buddha is free from all pain. He who pays homage to the Buddha or his disciples, who have crossed the flood of sorrow, acquires much merit.[3]

The Tirukkuṟaḷ[4] says that Dharma should be practised by one to the best of his ability. In the Dhammapada[5] a wise man always finds delight in Dhamma expounded by the Elect. He who is the drinker of Dhamma lives happily with a serene mind. Nothing is higher than Dhamma; to forget it is wrought with greatest evil. Do not cease to practise Dhamma on all possible occasions to the best of your ability. Happiness springs only from Dharma.[6] One who practises Dhamma lives happily in this world and in the next. One should practise Dhamma properly.[7]

If one practises righteousness daily he is not subject to rebirth.[8] Those who follow the law which has been well explained to them will overcome death.[9]

Be pure in mind. That is Dharma. All else is but pompous show. That course of conduct that steers clear of every desire, wrath and offensive speech, is alone Dharma. To do good and to avoid evil must be the law of our being.[10] Not to commit any sin, to do good and to purify one's mind - that is the teaching of the Awakened.[11] One should follow the law of virtue and should not follow that of sin.[12]

There is no greater life if it is free from reproach. The householder who keeps others in the right path and himself does not deviate from his, does greater penance than anchorites.[13] It is the supreme virtue of a householder to fulfil his obligations to his ancestors, gods, guests, relatives and himself.[14] A wise man should be watchful regarding himself. Let him direct himself first to what is proper, and then let him teach others. If evil is not done by oneself, he or she is purified.[15] One is sanctified if his speech be holy. He who forestalls blame is one who is restrained by modesty in all the world.[16] A true brahmin, although he has committed no offence, is one who can endure reproach. According to the Buddhist ideas instead of being free from reproach, if he can endure it without having committed any offence, he will thereby make him perfect.[17]

A woman, if she is chaste, is regarded as great.[18] A monk is worthy of being a monk if he remains chaste and if he is above good and evil.[19] Misconduct (duccaritam) is the flaw of a woman like stinginess in the case of a donor, and evil things are undoubtedly flaws both in this world and in the next.[20]

A life devoid of love is barren. If one's heart is devoid of love his outward feature becomes free from grace.[21] It may be applied to the case of the disciples of Gotama also who, according to the Dhammapada,[22] are always wide awake and find delight in non-harming day and night.

Virtue grows in one who speaks kind, sweet and inoffensive words.[23] In the Dhammapada[24], a monk is one who utters sweet words, who holds his mouth under control, who speaks the mantra, who is not arrogant, and who teaches weal and Dhamma. In the Tirukkural it is stated that a man knowing the pleasure that sweet speech gives, should not use harsh words.[25] According to the Dhammapada[26] harsh words should not be spoken to any man, for he may reply in the same manner. Provocative talk gives pain and retaliation may take place.

A wise man holds the scales evenly unminful of prosperity or adversity.[27] A wise man makes no show of ups and downs either in happiness or in sorrow.[28]

In the Tirukkuṛaḷ[29] the wealth of the upright never dwindles but it passes on to posterity. Give up ill-gotten wealth, though it brings prosperity. In the Dhammapada[30] he who does not desire his own prosperity by dishonest means, is virtuous and wise. One should not covet other's wealth for evils come out of convetousness[31]. One should not desire wealth for his own self or for others.[32] He who desires prosperity by dishonest means is not wise, virtuous and righteous. One should take care that greediness and vice do not bring him to grief for a long time.[33] A person earns wealth for rendering help to the deserving.[34] The Dhammapada deprecates thirst for wealth.[35] It states that wealth slays a wicked person but not those whose quest is the beyond. A wicked person on account of his thirst for wealth not only kills himself but also kills others.

In the Tirukkural[36] we find that whatever else you may not control, control your tongue lest you should repent for your indiscreet words. A word of evil will lead one to trouble. One will surely lose the fruit of his good deeds if he utters the word of evil. In the Dhammapada[37] one should control his tongue. He should give up all offence in speech and should be careful in not using angry words. He should also practise virtue with his speech. In the Tirukkural[38] the god of righteousness loves one who is above anger and attains self-control through knowledge. In the Dhammapada[39] those sages who do not harm anybody and who are always well-restrained in body go to the place where there is no death and where there is no grief.

Right conduct exalts a person.[40] He who is possessed of good conduct and insight (siladassana) is dear to us.[41] Good conduct brings happiness and bad conduct leads one to misery.[42]

One should strive hard to walk in the right path.[43] The Dhammapada[44] points out that the eightfold path is the best. This is the way towards the attainment of purity. One will put an end to suffering after reaching the right path.

In the Dhammapada[45] one who does a sinful act suffers in this world and in the next. One who does a good deed finds delight in this world and in the next. He is pleased looking at the purity of his deed. An evil doer suffers at the thought that an evil deed has been done by him. He suffers all the more after having gone to hell. A doer of a meritorious deed is pleased here and in the next. He is pleased at the thought that a meritorious deed has been done by him. He is pleased all the more after having reached the blessed region.

In the Tirukkural[46] the envious do not prosper. The wise do not commit any wrong out of envy, for they know the evils arising out of it.[47] In the Dhammapada[48] one should put away conceit[49] (manam). It is the aspiration of a fool that both the laymen and monks should think that this has been done by him and that what is to be done or not to be done should be deferred to him. His wishes and conceit grow (iccha mano ca vaddhati). Even the gods envy him who is free from pride and free from sins.[50] The Buddhas are free from vanity, but the world delights in vanity. Those who are sages do not harm anybody.[51] One should not envy others. Fortune forsakes the envious. Envy which is a deadly sin leads one to hell. Envy never thrives. Fortune never forsakes one who is free from envy. An envious, stingy, and dishonest man does not become good by talking too much or by the excellence of his complexion.[52]

In the Tirukkural[53] adultery should not be indulged in. In the Dhammapada[54] one should not visit other's wife because the king inflicts severe punishment. Those who visit other's wives get four things: (1) demerit, (2) uncomfortable bed (i.e. not getting rest), (3) blame, and (4) hell.[55] Misconduct is the woman's flaw. It is an evil thing both in this world and in the next.[56] The life of a shameless man is easy to live.[57] For one who ever seeks the pure, being detached and not assertive, pure in life, life is hard to live.[58]

If one wishes to maintain character one's conduct must be marked by patience.[59] Patience is the supreme austerity (khanti param tapo).[60] He who patiently bears harsh words, is the trained man who is the best among men.[61] In the Tirukkural.[62] One should forbear the harm done to him by another. In the Dhammapada,[63] the Buddha says that forbearance is the excellent waning out.

One who endures the insolent words of the transgressor is greater than an ascetic.[64] In the Dhammapada[65] he is not a recluse who does injury to another. One who has renounced the world does no harm to others.

In the Dhammapada[66] contentment does not lie in sense-desires. The wise know that sense-desires are sufferings and distasteful.[67] One does not find delight even in celestial sense-desires. A learned man (pandito) should give up sensual pleasures.[68] Delightful are the forests where the people come not to take pleasure; they will find delight being free from passion; they are not in search for sensual pleasures.[69] Those who move about being alert for beauty, unrestrained in senses, immoderate in food, slothful and inert, are easily overcome by Mara the sinner.[70]

In the Tirukkural[71] one should not be guilty of slander. In the Dhammapada[72] if one finds fault with others and always of captious mind, his own sins grow. Men blame the silent sitter, they also blame the much talker, they also blame those who talk moderately. There is none in this world who is not blamed. There is none in this world who is solely blamed or who is solely praised.[73] The wise remain unmoved either by praise or by blame.[74]

In the Tirukkural[75] he who utters silly words is despised by all. It is better not to utter empty words.[76] A good man will never indulge in vain words.[77] A well uttered speech becomes fruitless if it is not carried into action and vice versa.[78]

One does not become learned and righteous by talking much. He should guard his speech. A monk should be restrained in his speech. He who holds his speech under control utters sweet words.[79]

One should be afraid of evil deed. If one really loves oneself, he or she should not do any harm to others. Sorrow hardly comes to a person who does not deviate from right.[80] A man should entirely avoid evil things. One should repel his mind from evil deed. Suffering comes from evil. The fool who offends the person who is pure and free from fault, suffers from the very evil. Those who perform sinful deeds go to hell. One cannot escape from evil deed whether he may be in the sky, or in the mid-ocean, or in the hill-cave. Evil does not come to a person who has not done anything wrong.

Far nobler than one thousand oblations to fire is an act of abstinence from taking flesh.[81] One should not kill anybody or cause another person to kill, making his own self type, because life is dear to all.[82] One does not become an elect because he kills living creatures. One becomes so by avoiding life-slaughter.[83] One becomes a true brahmin who does not kill nor cause slaughter.[84]

Non-killing is the sum-total of virtues. Do not commit any act of violence.[85] A man is called an elect because he has pity on all living creatures and because he does not injure them.[86] He is not just if he carries a matter by violence.[87]

Nothing lasts except one's fearless renown.[88] One who is blessed with fame and riches, is honoured wherever he goes.[89] The scent of the pious goes against the wind. A good man pervades all directions. Odour of virtue is supreme among all sorts of perfumes.[90]

The unblemished truly live.[91] One becomes a true brahmin if he is blameless.[92] One should be compassionate.[93] A monk who behaves with compassion is sure to reach Nirvana.[94]

True charity lies in the gift to the poor alone.[95] The gift of Dhamma conquers all gifts.[96]

The weak should not be oppressed.[97] One should be cordial in his ways and one should be righteous in his deeds.[98] This is applicable not only to the monks but also to the laity. One should not expect any return for the service done.[99]

The Dhammapada does not contain the idea that nothing should be expected in return for the serive done. But in the verse 166 it is pointed out that a person should not neglect his own duty for the sake of another's welfare, however great. He should always be attentive to his duty after knowing it.

The true form of penance is to put up with all pains and to abstain from injury.[100] In the Dhammapada[101] penance is the supreme austerity. He is not a recluse who strikes and insults others. Penance is only possible for the disciplined.[102] Men who have not observed proper discipline, perish.[103]

A man loses his saintly behaviour if his mind is bent on evil.[104] He is advised to avoid evil deeds.[105] If he commits any sin, let him not do it again, because the accumulation of evil is painful.[106] If a man does what is good, let him do it again, because the accumulation of good is delightful.[107] One should not think lightly of evil. A fool becomes full of evil even if he gathers it little by little.[108] An evil-doer sees happiness so long as his evil deed does not ripen. But when his evil deed becomes ripe, then the evil-doer sees it.[109] It is quite clear from the Dhammapada (Ch. IX) that an evil-doer really loses his saintliness. If persons abstain from evil deeds there is no need either for tonsure or for matted locks.[110] He is a true brahmana when he is rid of evil. He does not offend by deed, word or thought.[111] For a fool it is no good having plaited hair. His inside is dirty. It is no good cleaning outside.[112]

He who wants to command respect must guard his mind against robbing others.[113] Those who know stealing only will indulge in an unrighteous act and will forthwith perish.[114] He who takes what is not given him brings about his own ruin.[115] A true brahmin is one who takes nothing in the world that is not given him.[116] One should be truthful.[117] He who is endowed with truth, temperate, free from sins and virtuous, is indeed worthy of yellow robe.[118] They who know truth in truth and untruth in untruth arrive at truth.[119] One should banish anger from his mind.[120] Do not get angry with anyone.[121] He who restrains his anger shows real restraint.[122] Men given to anger are the companions of the devil, and those who are free from it live with the immortals.[123] One should give up anger.[124] One should not yield to it.[125] He who holds back rising anger like a rolling chariot is called a real charioteer.[126] He will go near the gods by removing anger.[127] If one fails to control bodily anger, anger of the tongue, and anger of the mind, he is sure to suffer.[128]

It is a supreme virtue not to do even the slightest injury to others.[129] Avoid all that causes pain to others.[130] One should not commit any sin but he should do good to others.[131] One should not strike others causing injury.[132] It is further enjoined by the Dhammapada[133], that a man should hasten towards the good and keep his thought away from evil. Evil-doers go to hell, and the righteous people go to heaven.[134]

One should properly understand what is stable and what is unstable.[135] A true brahmin is one who is thoughtful, steady, free from doubts, free from attachment, and who has reached the other shore.[136]

A man does not suffer pain from renunciation. Ascetics renounce the world.[137] One should cut off all attachments.[138] One should seek refuge in him who is free from desires.[139] One should dig up the root of thirst.[140] Wise people cut off the fetter and leave the world, free from cares.[141] He is a true brahmin who is free from all attachments although he may be poor.[142] He is a true brahmin who has abandoned all his longings.[143] One is a true brahmana whose passions are extinct, i.e. who has subdued his senses.[144] A monk is really freed form all pain.[145] One should give up his longings. There is no sorrow from those who are free from desires.[146] One becomes happy when his desire dies out.[147] Ascetics fear desires.[148] When a person overcomes his thirst, he becomes free from sufferings.[149] The extinction of thirst overcomes all pain.[150] The root of thirst should be removed.[151] A just person has obtained confidence because he has obtained the extinction of desires.[152] One cannot be an ascetic if he is given up to desire and greediness.[153]

Men of pure vision dispel darkness. One should seek the truth to remove delusion.[154] One should do away with lust, anger and delusion which lead to rebirth.[155] He in whom there exist truth, virtue, pity, restraint, moderation, wisdom, and freedom from impurity is called an elder.[156] Mankind is ruined by passion, hatred, delusion and lust. A gift bestowed on the passionless and on those who are free from hatred, delusion and lust, bring great reward.[157]

One should speak the truth and make a gift, however small, and thereby he will go near the gods.[158]

Pleasure and pain are all the workings of fate.[159] They who see sin where there is no sin and see no sin where there is sin, such men embracing the false doctrine enter the evil path wherein lies suffering. They who see sin where there is sin and no sin where there is no sin, such men embracing the right doctrine enter the good path wherein lies happiness.[160] Not done is better than ill-done, ill-done afterwards brings pain; a good deed is better done, for having done it one does not repent.[161]

The duty of the learned is to delight men by their comapny. The precious wealth of a man is his learning.[162] The learned man who shows you what is to be avoided, should be followed.[163] Let him admonish, teach, forbid what is improper, he will be beloved of the good.[164]

Wisdom saves one from evil.[165] A wise man should be watchful. If a man holds himself dear, let him watch himself carefully. A wise man will not suffer because he will see what is proper.[166] Wisdom of a child is not only the delight of his father but also the delight of the whole world.[167] It is pleasant to have attained wisdom.[168]

The world lives through kindliness.[169] The disciples of Gautam always find delight in compasion.[170] The monk who behaves with kindness, who is happy with the doctrine of the Buddha, will reach Nirvana.[171]

Exertion is one's real possession.[172] It is one's wealth, and it is one's strength. Earnestness is the path of Nirvana.[173] Those who are earnest do not die. By earnestness vanity can be removed.[174] He who is earnest and meditative obtains ample joy.[175] Earnestness is always praised. By earnestness Indra attained the lordship of gods.[176] A monk who delights in earnestness, moves about like fire burning all fetters.[177]

Slothfulness should never be encouraged.[178] It is always blamed.[179] A wise monk should keep noble friends whose life is pure and who are not slothful.[180]

According to the Tirukkural a man's friends bring prosperity to him.[181] It is easy for one to say but it is difficult to do.[182] The friend of the wise resembles the waxing crescent; the friendship of the unwise fades like the waning moon.[183] Better to have solitude than the aliance of the wicked.[184] Better to abandon than make friendship with the low people who do not help you in adversity.[185] It is wise to avoid friendship with those who befriend you at home but betray you in the public.[186] The stupid people are shameless, negligent and arrogant.[187] Hatred is a foul disease that brings discord among men.[188] Out of modesty springs one's greatness.[189] Greatness is all humility.[190] Good conduct is the virtue of the great.[191] The noble would rather die than lose modesty.[192] Ignoble men envy others and slander them.[193]

Friends who have stood by you in hour of sorrow should not be abandoned.[194] According to the Dhammapada[195], one should serve good friends and not bad friends. The friendship of virtuous men should be secured.[196] The company of the wicked is the greatest evil.[197] One should not have wicked people as his friends.[198] He who walks in the company of fools suffers.[199]

According to the Dhammapada one cannot lead a holy life if he talks much that is proper but he seldom acts accordingly.[200] The words of a person who does not act accordingly, are furitless although they are fine. The words of a person who acts accordingly, are both fine and furitful.[201] If an intelligent man be associated only for a minute with a wise man, he will soon perceive the truth.[202] If a fool be associated with a wise man throughout his life, it would be difficult for him to perceive the truth.[203] If a traveller does not meet with one who is his better or his equal, let him firmly keep to his solitary journey.[204] One should not have low people for friends.[205] He who walks in the company of fools suffers a long way; company with fools as with an enemy is always painful.[206] The Dhammapada gives the characteristic of the stupid people who are described as fools in several places. It refers to them as thoughtless people. Those who are thoughtless are as if dead.[207] A thoughtless man has no share in the priesthood, but he is like a cowherd counting the cows of others.[208] The fools are described as men of evil wisdom who follow after vanity.[209] The fool who knows his foolishness is wise so far, but a fool who thinks himself wise is called a fool indeed.[210] An evil deed follows the fool.[211] There is no shark like hatred.[212] Hatred does not cease by hatred at any time; it ceases by love.[213] When any evil thought is not harboured, hatred will cease.[214] Life is easy to live for a man who is shameless, mischief-maker, bold, an insulting and wretched fellow.[215] Life is hard to live for a modest man who always looks to purity, who is unselfish, quiet, spotless and intelligent.[216] Good conduct is pleasant, lasting till old age.[217] A man does not become noble by doing injury to others. An envious, stingy and dishonest man does not become respectable by means of much talking or by the beauty of his complexion.[218]

Notes and References

1. Tirukkural, vv, 4,7,10.
2. Dhammapada, vv. 190, 192
3. Dh., vv. 196, 196
4. T., v.33.
5. Dh. v. 79; Cf. Milinda, 345.
6. T., vv. 32, 33, 39.
7. Dh., v. 168; Cf. Milinda, 213.
8. T., v. 38.
9. Dh., v. 86; Cf. Anguttara V.232
10. T., vv. 34, 35, 40.
11. Dh., v.183; Cf. Digha, ii, 49; Netti, 43, 81, 171, 186, Mahavastu, iii, 420.
12. Dh. v. 169,Cf. Avadanasataka, Ed. speyer, Vol.I, pp.220 & 222.
13. T., vv. 48, 49.
14. T., vv. 43.
15. Dh., vv. 157, 158, 165.
16. Dh., vv. 96, 143.
17. Dh. v.399.
18. T., v. 54.
19. Dh.v. 267; Cf. Samyutta, I, 182.
20. Dh., v. 242; Cf.Ang. IV. 195.
21. T., vv. 78-79.
22. Dh., v. 300.
23. T., vv. 96-98
24. Dh., v. 363; Cf. Suttanipata, 850.
25. T.,v. 99,
26. Dh., v. 133.
27. T., v. 115
28. Dh., v. 83.
29. T., vv.112, 173.
30. Dh., v.84.
31. T., v. 177.
32. Dh., v. 84.
33. Dh., v. 248.
34. T.,v. 219.
35. Dh., v. 355.
36. T.vv. 127, 128.

37. Dh., v.232.
38. T., v.130.
39. Dh., v. 225.
40. T. v. 131.
41. Dh., v. 217.
42. T.,v. 138.
43. T., v. 132.
44. Dh., vv. 274-275.
45. Dh., vv. 15-18.
46. T.,v. 135.
47. Ibid., v. 164.
48. Dh., v. 221.
49. Cf. Sam, I, 23.
50. Cf. Netti, 162.
51. Dh., vv. 74,94, 254,225.
52. T.,vv. 161, 167, 168, 170; Cf.Dh., v.262.
53. Ibid., v.150.
54. Dh., v.310.
55. Ibid., v.309.
56. Ibid., v. 242.
57. Ibid., v. 244.
58. Dh., v. 245.
59. T., v.154.
60. Dh., v. 184.
61. Ibid., v.321.
62. T., v. 158.
63. Dh., v. 184.
64. T., v. 159.
65. Dh., v. 184.
66. Ibid., vv. 186-187.
67. Cf. Vinaya, ii, 25; Divya, 224.
68. Dh., v.88.
69. Dh., v. 99.
70. Ibid., v.7.
71. T., v. 181.
72. Dh., v.253.
73. Dh., vv. 227, 228.
74. Ibid., v.81; Vin. I, 185; Milinda, 386.
75. T.,v. 191.
76. Ibid., v.194.

77. Ibid., v.196
78. Dh., vv. 51, 52.
79. Dh., vv. 258, 259, 281, 361, 363.
80. T., vv. 202, 209, 210.
81. T.,v. 259.
82. Dh., vv. 123, 116, 117, 125, 126, 127, 124, 129, 130; Netti, 130; Jat, III, 292; Divyav, 339.
83. Dh., v. 270
84. Ibid., v.405
85. T., 321, 327.
86. Dh., v.270.
87. Ibid., v.256.
88. T., v.233.
89. Dh., v.303.
90. Ibid., vv. 54, 55; Cf. Ang., I.226; Milinda, 933.
91. T., v.240.
92. Dh., 386, 388
93. T., v., 242.
94. Dh., v. 368; Mahavastu, III, 421, 523.
95. T., v. 221.
96. Dh., v.354.
97. T., v.250.
98. Dh., v.376.
99. T.,v. 211.
100. T.,v. 261.
101. Dh., v.184; Digha. ii, 49.
102. T., v. 263.
103. Dh., v. 155.
104. T.,v. 272.
105. Dh., v. 123.
106. Ibid., v.117.
107. T., v. 188.
108. Dh., v. 121; Cf.Jat.III, 169.
109. Dh.,v. 119.
110. T.,v. 280.
111. Dh., vv. 388-391; Cf. Netti, p.183.
112. Dh., v. 394.
113. T., v.281.
114. Ibid., v. 289.
115. Dh., v.246.

116. Ibid., 409.
117. T., v.297.
118. Dh., v. 10; Jat. II, 198.
119. Dh., v.12.
120. T.,v. 309.
121. Ibid., v.303.
122. Ibid., v.301.
123. Ibid., v.310.
124. Dh., v.221.
125. Dh., v. 224.
126. Ibid., v.222.
127. Ibid., v.224.
128. Ibid., vv. 231-233.
129. T., v.317.
130. Ibid., v. 316.
131. Dh., v. 183; Digha, II. 49; Mahavastu, III, 420.
132. Dh., v. 185; Udana, IV, 490.
133. Dh., v. 116; Jat, IV, 490.
134. Dh., v. 126; Mahav. II, 424.
135. T.V. 331.
136. Dh., v.414; Cf. Ang. iv. 290.
137. T.vv. 341, 314.
138. T.,v. 349.
139. T.v., 350.
140. Dh., v. 337; Cf. Dh., v.216; Netti, p.42; Jataka, iii, 387.
141. Dh.,v. 346.
142. Ibid., v.396.
143. Ibid., v. 416.
144. Ibid., v.420.
145. Dh., v. 361; Sam, I,73; Milinda, 399.
146. T., vv. 368, 370.
147. Ibid., v.369.
148. Ibid., v.366.
149. Dh., v.336. It is also stated in the Dhammapada that sorrow and fear come from the beloved. When one becomes free from the beloved, he has neither sorrow nor fear. Dh.,v.212; Cf. Avadanasataka Ed. by J.S.Spreyer; Vol.I.191.
150. Dh.,v. 354.
151. Ibid., v.337.
152. Dh., vv. 271-72; Mahav, iii, 422.

153. Dh., v. 264.
154. T., vv. 352, 358.
155. Ibid., v.860.
156. Dh., v. 261.
157. Ibid., vv. 356-59.
158. Dh., v. 224.
159. T., v.379.
160. Dh., vv. 318-19.
161. Dh., v.314.
162. T.,vv. 394. 400.
163. Dh., v.76; Theragatha, 993.
164. Dh., v. 77; Theragatha, 994.
165. T., v.421.
166. Dh., vv. 157-58.
167. T., v.68.
168. Dh., v.333; Sukho pannaya patilabho.
169. T., v. 572.
170. Dh., v.300.
171. Ibid., v. 368; Mahavastu, iii, 421, 523.
172. T., vv. 591, 592, 600.
173. Dh., v.21; Netti, 34.
174. Dh., v.28; Milinda, 387.
175. Dh., v.27; Theragatha, 883-4.
176. Dh., v.30; Sam.I. 229.
177. Dh., v.31.
178. T., v.602.
179. Dh., v.30.
180. Dh., v.375.
181. T., v.651.
182. T., v.664.
183. T.,v. 781.
184. Ibid., 814.
185. Ibid., 816.
186. Ibid., v. 820.
187. Ibid.,v. 833.
188. Ibid., v.851.
189. Ibid., v.960.
190. Ibid., v.978.
191. Ibid.,v.982.
192. Ibid., v.1017.

193. Ibid., v.1079.
194. T., v.106.
195. Dh., v.78; Cf.v.207; T., v.106.
196. T., v.441; Cf.Dh. v.78.
197. T.,v. 460.
198. Dh., v. 78.
199. Dh., v.207.
200. Ibid., v. 19.
201. Ibid., vv. 51-52; Therag. 323-24.
202. Dh., v.65.
203. Ibid., v.64.
204. Ibid., v.61.
205. Ibid., v. 78.
206. Dh., v. 207.
207. Ibid., v.21.
208. Ibid., v.19.
209. Ibid., v.26.
210. Ibid., v.63.
211. Ibid., v. 71; Netti, 161.
212. Dh., v.251.
213. Dh., v.5.
214. Dh., v.4.
215. Dh., v.244.
216. Ibid., v.245.
217. Ibid., v.333.
218. Ibid., v.270.

Select Bibliography

Ahir, D.C., *Buddhist Shrines in India*, Delhi, 1986.

Heritage of Buddhism, Delhi, 1989.

Aiyangar, S. Krishnaswami, *Manimekhalai in its Historical Setting*, London, 1928.

History of Tirupati, Vol. I, Madras, 1940.

Ancient India and the South Indian History and Culture, Poona, 1941.

Aiyar, S.K.V., *Historical Sketches of Ancient Deccan*, 1917, New Delhi, 1987.

Bagchi, P.C., *India and China*, Calcutta, 1944.

Banerjee, A.C., *Buddhism in India and Abroad*, Calcutta, 1973.

Bapat, P.V. Ed., *2500 Years of Buddhism*, Delhi, 1956, 1987.

Barua, Dipak Kumar, *Viharas in Ancient India*, Calcutta, 1969.

Basham, A.L., *The Wonder that was India*, Calcutta,1974.

Beal, Samuel, *SI-Yu-Ki Buddhist Records of the Western World* - translated from the Chinese of Hiuen Tsiang, Delhi, 1981 edition.

Bhattacharya, N.N., *Ancient History and Civilization*, New Delhi, 1988.

Burgess, J., *Archaeological Survey of India Volume IV*, Report of the Buddhist Cave Temples and their Inscriptions, London, 1883.

Cunningham, Alexander, *Ancient Geography of India,* edited by S.N. Majumdar, Calcutta, 1924, Reprint Varanasi, 1963.

Dasgupta, S.N., *A History of Indian Philosophy,* Volume II, 1961.

Dhammaratana, H., *Buddhism in South India,* Buddhist Publication Society, Kandy, Ceylon, 1968.

Dutt, R.C., *Buddhism and Buddhist Civilization in India,* New Delhi, 1983.

Fausball, V., *The Sacred Books of the East,* The Sutta Nipata - translated from Pali, Delhi, reprint, 1973.

Ghoshal, U.N., *Studies in Indian History and Culture,* Bombay, 1957.

Gopalan, R., *History of Pallavas of Kanchi,* Madras, 1928 .

Gopinatha Rao, T.A., *Elements of Hindu Iconography,* Madras, 1924.

Buddhist Vestiges in Kanchipuram, Indian Antiquary, Vol. XLIV.

Vestiges of Buddhism and Jainism in Kerala.

Hazra, K.L., *Royal Patronage of Buddhism,* Delhi, 1984.

Joshi, L.M., *Studies in Buddhist Culture of India,* Delhi, 1967.

Kosambi, D.D., *The Culture and Civilization of Ancient India in Historical Outline,* New Delhi, 1976.

Kulkarni, A.R., *Buddha The Trimurti and Modern Hinduism,* Nagpur, 1980.

Lama Chimpa, Alka Chattopadhyaya Edited by Debiprasad Chattopadhayaya., *Taranatha's History of India,* Simla, 1970.

Ludders, H., *A List of Brahmi Inscriptions Appendix to Epigraphica Indica and Record of the Archaeological Survey of India,* Volume X, Calcutta, 1969.

Law, B.C., *Indological Studies,* Part II, Calcutta, 1942.

Mahalingam, T.V., *Kanchipuram in early South Indian History*, Madras, 1954.

Majumdar, R.C., *History and Culture of the Indian People, Vol. II, The Age of Imperial Unity*, Bombay, 1951.

History and Culture of the Indian People, Vol. III. The Classical Age, Bombay, 1954.

Ancient India, Delhi reprint, 1986.

Maurice Winterintz, *A History of Indian Literature, Vol. II, Buddhist Literature and Jaina Literatures*, Delhi, 1983.

Mitra, Mrs Debala, *Buddhist Monuments*, Calcutta, 1971.

Mookerji, Rakha Kumud, *Asoka*, Delhi reprint, 1986.

Nalinaksha Dutt, *Buddhist Sects in India*, Delhi, 1977.

Mahayana Buddhism, Calcutta, 1973.

Narasu, P. Lakshmi, *The Essence of Buddhism*, Madras, 1911, Delhi, 1948.

Narain, A.K. Ed., *Studies in History of Buddhism*, Delhi, 1976.

Nilakanta Sastrai, K.A., *History of India*, Madras, 1950.

Foreign Notices of South India.

A History of South India, Madras, 1984, edition.

Parameswaran Pillai, V.R., *Temple Culture of South India*, New Delhi, 1986.

Pillai, Vaijayapuri, S., History of *Tamil Language and Literature*, Madras, 1956.

Padmanabha Menon, K.P. Ed. T.K. Krishna Menon, *History of Kerala*, Volume I, New Delhi, 1982 edition.

Rajasekhara, S., *Early Chalukyan Art at Aiholi*, New Delhi, 1985.

Ramanan, K.V., Nagarj*una's Philosophy*, Varanasi, 1971.

Ramamurthy, V., *History of Kongu*, Madras, 1986.

Ramaswamy, A., *History of Pondicherry*, New Delhi, 1987.

Ramaswami, N.S., *Indian Monuments*, New Delhi, 1979.

Ramesan, N., *Temples and Legends of Andhra.*

Raychaudhuri, H.C., *Political History of Ancient,* India, Calcutta, 1953.

Rhys Davids, T.W., *Buddhist India*, Delhi reprint, 1971.

Sangharakshita, Bhikshu, *A Survey of Buddhism*, Bangalore, 1976.

Sarkar, H. and S.P. Nainar, *Amaravati*, Archaeological Survey, of India, New Delhi, 1980.

Sarkar, H. and B.N. Misra, *Nagarjunakonda*, Archaeological Survey of India, New Delhi, 1980.

Sarma, I.K., *Studies in Early Buddhist Monuments Brahmi Inscriptions of Andhra Desa*, Nagpur, 1988.

Sathianata Aiyer, R., *Studies in the Ancient History of Tondamandalam*, Madras, 1944.

Seshagiri Rao, B., *Studies in South Indian Jainism*, Delhi, 1982.

Shetty, Vasantha B., *Studies in Karnataka History*, New Delhi, 1984.

Sircar, D.C., *Inscriptions of Asoka*, Delhi, 1952.

Sivaraja Pillai, K.N., *The Chronology of the Early Tamils*, Madras, 1932, New Delhi, 1984.

Sivaramamurti, C., *Amaravati Sculptures in the Madras Government Museum*, Madras, 1977.

Smith, V.A., *Asoka*, Oxford, 1924.

Sreedhara Menon, A., *Cultural Heritage of Kerala*, Cochin, 1978.

Srinivasan, C.R., *Kanchipuram Through the Ages*, New Delhi, 1979.

Srinivasan, K.R., *Temples of South India*, New Delhi, 1979.

Srinivasan, P.R., *Story of Buddhism with Special Reference to South India*, Madras, 1960.

Subramanian, K.R., *Buddhist Remains in Andhra*, Madras, 1932.

Subramanian, N., *History of Tamilnad*, Madurai, 1972.

Thapar, Romila, *Asoka and the Decline of the Mauryas*, Delhi, 1973.

Vaidyanathan, K.R., *Temples and Legands of Kerala*, Bombay, 1982.

Venkataraman, R., *Indian Archaeology - A Survey*, Madras, 1985.

Watters, Thomas, *On Yuan Chwang's Travels in India*, Delhi reprint, 1961.

Yazdani, G., *Early History of Deccan*, London, 1960.

Index

(A) GENERAL

(B) STATE-WISE

Andhra Pradesh

Karnataka

Kerala

Pondicherry

Tamil Nadu

Two Buddha's Statues in the village of Pallu,Kanchipuram, Tamil Nadu

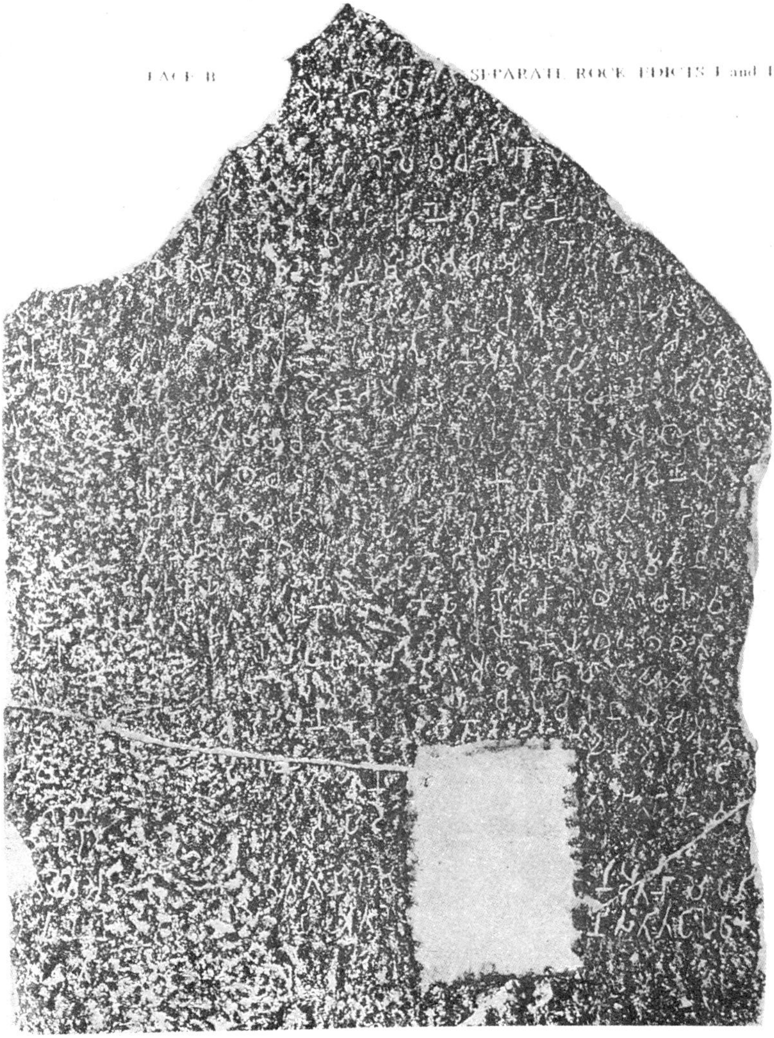

Ashokan Rock Edict at Sanati, Gulbarga Dist., Karnataka

Chaitya-griha with Buddha,Nagarjunakonda, [illegible]